SALES ENABLEMENT 3.0 ENDORSEMENTS

In *Sales Enablement 3.0* Roderick Jefferson explains why Sales Enablement hasn't evolved in 20 years and why that is squandering the potential of millions of salespeople worldwide. He explains what sales enablement's obsession with measuring the wrong metrics is doing to slow down sales, reduce profits and harm close rates. More importantly, he provides the blueprint required to make the changes.

—Marcus Cauchi, CRO, hypergrowth expert, author of *Making Channel Sales Work*

"Sales enablement can be a tremendous positive or the ultimate blocker to a company's success. It can often seem like a black art. Roderick Jefferson is a star in the field and offers the most practical and actionable sales enablement tutorial that I have seen."

—Tom Mendoza, Former Chairman and President, NetApp

"*Enablement 3.0* is a masterclass for those wanting to transform their sales enablement efforts into being a trusted partner for any business. The visual presentations are worth the price of the book! Roderick has taken literally decades of experiences and reduced them into an easy to read, highly relevant playbook of best practices. Whether you are launching sales enablement in a startup or supporting scalable growth for a large enterprise, this book will help you and your team."

—Tim Ohai, Global Director, Sales Enablement, Workday

"Today's buyers are more savvy, knowledgeable, and prepared than ever. That means the way we sell, communicate, and engage with our customers must evolve. In Sales Enablement 3.0, Roderick reminds us what is most important for any sales organization - knowing your buyer. Through his Focus, Unite, Adjust and Incorporate strategy you will learn how to transform your
and ultimately the way you sell. It's tin
to begin!

—Daryl Spreiter, Sales E

"This book is a blueprint, written based upon the real-world experience of what does and does not work. It is also a guide for enablement practitioners and leaders looking to take the journey from sales enablement to revenue enablement, from sales-centric to customer-centric by supporting the entire go-to-market team, driving increased revenue, decreasing churn, and reducing risk in the process, they earn their seat at the executive table."

—John Moore, The Collaborator,
VP of Revenue Enablement, Bigtincan

Sales Enablement 3.0 serves as a roadmap for existing, emerging, and aspiring sales enablement practitioners. Roderick does a masterful job of breaking down the essential elements of building a thriving sales enablement culture, sharing anecdotes, and insightful experiences, while framing the adapting mindset required to harmonize sales enablement as a profession. Sales Enablement 3.0 is a manifestation of his vision, commitment, and leadership in our profession.

—Ed Ross, CEO,
Michigan & Manchester Consulting Group/CoreAi

"*Sales Enablement 3.0* is an insightful, innovative blueprint that simplifies and demystifies the art & science of sales enablement. The author is a leading, international sales enablement expert. Read this action-packed book! It offers a rich perspective that will enhance your approach to sales enablement."

—Gerhard Gschwandtner, CEO, Selling Power Magazine

"Roderick has authored a book that clearly defines what the future of Sales Enablement is and is not. He shares his wisdom on the subject in an easy to understand format that is both practical and relevant to real-world situations. This is a highly valuable book for any B2B leader looking to significantly improve the company's sales productivity."

—Jeff Davis, B2B Growth Strategist,
author of *Create Togetherness*

"Roderick's book, *Sales Enablement 3.0* is a must read for business and corporate leadership. He writes, "It is time to shift our mindset away from the old premise of training. Training is a single, one-time event with little to no reinforcement. While training is a component of enablement, it is just one of many components." What I truly value is that his message isn't the latest or greatest or the next sales fad. This book is filled with evergreen principles that will provide value to this and the next generation of sales professionals.

—Keith Wolaridge, Principal, Wolaridge Consulting, Author of *Five Pillars*

Sales Enablement 3.0

Sales Enablement 3.0

The Blueprint to Sales Enablement Excellence

RODERICK JEFFERSON

If you would like to purchase bulk copies of Sales Enablement 3.0: The Blueprint to Sales Enablement Excellence, please contact Roderick Jefferson & Associates, LLC at info@roderickjefferson.com or www.roderickjefferson.com/contact for a pricing quote.

PRINTED IN THE UNITED STATES OF AMERICA

This book is dedicated to:

Debra, Tiffannie and Nate Jefferson
Shirley Johnson
Janet Thompson
Penny "Aunt Peg" Haynes
Madies Jean "The Purple Lady" Futrell
Lois Jean Lovelace
Joyce Powell

Thank you for grooming and shaping me into the person,
leader, and sales enablement professional that I am today.
There were many times that I wanted to give up and walk away
from writing this book, but you refused to allow me to do it.
Thank you for your loving words of encouragement, validation,
and occasional kick in the pants!

And also:
Thank you to all of my family members, extended family
members, tribe of friends, colleagues, fellow speakers, authors, team-
mates, mentors, and sponsors who have believed in my
vision for the Sales Enablement 3.0 framework from the beginning.
Your continued support is what pushed me to write this book.

IN HONORARIUM

Jim Ninavaggi, thank you for being my mentor, role model, and friend. You were one of the godfathers of sales enablement. I do not have the words to express the value and importance of the Sales Enablement Program of the Year award that you presented me with at the SiriusDecisions conference. It was hard to tell who was more excited about it, you or me. More importantly, thank you for teaching me how to focus on who I am versus what I do. The world is infinitely and eternally better because you were a part of it. You are missed, my friend!

CONTENTS

ACKNOWLEDGMENTS

I had no idea how many people it took to write and publish a book. If you like the content and stories in this book, the following people should get the credit; if you do not like it, the blame sits squarely on my shoulders.

First and foremost, thank you to Janet Thompson for teaching me how to double click. Little did I realize that your patience, focus, dedication, and determination would become a pivotal moment in time that would change the path of my life forever!

HUGE thank yous to Rob Acker, Kevin Akeroyd, Valerie Allman, Fontella Armstrong, Max Aultschuler, Darrel Ballard, John Barrows, Adrienne Brannigan, Todd Caponi, Marcus Cauchi, Cheryl Christensen, Nitin Chitkara, Jeff Davis, Gaetano DiNardi, Sarah Fenner, Corey Frank, Carmela Jaravata, Natalina Gonzalez, Gerhard Gschwandtner, Robby Halford, Morgan Ingram, Orlando Harris, Richard Huang, Julianna Hynes, Morgan Ingram, Marian Jamme, Suhail Khan, Andy Korenak, Laurie Lambert, Larry Levine, Dave Lichtman, Tom Mendoza, John McKeague, Medina McKinney, Scott McNabb, John Moore, Garnor Morantes, Erick Mott, Toni Navy, Anita Nielsen, Tamera McMillen, Scott McNabb, Stephane McShane, Tim Ohai, Mark Parry, Sheryl Powers, Angela Pritchett, Brett Queener, Ronnell Richards, Ron Reis, Ed Ross, Tamera Schmidt, John Short, Tom Siebel, Daryl Spreiter, J. D. Stewart, Matt Swanson, Judy Tian, Darrel Walker, Donna Weber, R. J. Weigel, Keith Wolaridge, and Daryle Whyte.

Thanks for teaching me the ropes and always demanding that I "get comfortable with being uncomfortable" when my visions were viewed as unconventional and experimental. Your push for continued advancement and innovation were the driving forces behind my mind shift to up-level the profession to Sales Enablement 3.0!

HUGE thank you to my First Book Done Cohort (FBD) family, Connie Alleyne, Lyna Nyamwaya, Patryce Sheppard, Staci Scott, Carl Stokes, and Vania Swain, for listening to me week over week, during our Master Class, and never giving up on me. You have inspired me more than you will ever know to finally give birth to this book. I am eternally grateful, honored, and humbled.

Finally, a HUGE thank you to my book doula, mentor, and friend, Geovanni Derice, for your process, assistance, support, and dedication. Your patience, engagement, guidance, perseverance, and framework made what was an impossible task become a reality. I am forever indebted to you!

FOREWORD

Over my lifetime, I have had the joy and good fortune to have been surrounded by amazing leaders both personally and professionally. My father, a consummate salesman, reminded me my whole that, "Nothing happens until somebody sells something." It might seem overly simple but consider something as small as the plastic cap on the end of your shoelace, to a multi-million-dollar private jet, it all starts with a sale. The world will forever turn on the notion that transactions get consummated between someone with a quota who has intimate knowledge of the business challenges of a buyer and can describe enough empirical evidence of a potential positive outcome to justify the purchase of your goods and services and the buyer.

Since the beginning of the modern selling evolution in the 30's, we as sellers have been desperately seeking a way to hack the selling motion by trying to find a way to make it simple to buy, make the process definable, and push a buyer towards an outcome, often times without regard for the buyers' personal wins, whether we were even the right solution for the problem.

At no time in modern history has there been a more fundamental shift in the way buyers buy than in the last decade. The consumer is gravitating away from responding to sales approaches and methodologies that were conceived 50+ years ago, and they are doing so at lightspeed. We as sales professionals can choose to pivot with the buyer and get out in front of this shift or suffer the fate of the dinosaur. This is where the art and science of sales enablement needs to be applied.

In this book, *Sales Enablement 3.0: The Blueprint to Sales Enablement Excellence*, Roderick Jefferson provides sales enablement practitioners with the foundational tools and techniques required to enable the modern seller to not only embrace this shift but to anticipate and adjust our approach to market personas. Using these techniques, Roderick provides game-changing blueprint that the modern seller must have to repeatably win in an ever-changing climate. I have known and called Roderick my brother for well over 10 years. As a foundational pioneer of the modern sales enablement movement, Roderick and his unique approach will help sales enablement practitioners and sales professionals to up-level their game in a challenging sales climate.

W. Scott McNabb

Chief Revenue Officer, 20+ year SaaS Sales Expert,

USAF Veteran

INTRODUCTION

You train animals and you enable people.

It all started in 1995, when I began my first grown-up job working with AT&T as an inside sales representative. I did well in my first couple of years by creating a few basic, rudimentary templates that saved time and didn't require me to recreate the wheel with every new prospect or customer. Within two years I was promoted to account executive and named the Top eCommerce Sales Professional in my region. The best part about this award was that I won it by outselling seasoned veterans who had been in the region for years.

After a nomination to Sales President's Club, my regional vice president offered me the opportunity to move into a sales leadership role. I quickly rejected the offer. As any good sales professional would do, I countered with my "candy bar job," something I would do even if I was only paid in my favorite candy, Reese's Peanut Butter Cups. My candy bar job was as a regional trainer, which would give me the opportunity to share the tools, templates, and best practices that had made me successful across the region.

My counter-offer was accepted, and I went into this new job with two goals:

1. Create a role that would allow me to work within the sales organization without actually carrying a quota.
2. Make enough money to support my family and take nice vacations without having to worry about how we would pay the bills once the vacation ended.

Little did I know that this change in career path would become the foundation that my 25-year, award-winning career would be built upon. I have been extremely fortunate to design, build, deploy, and lead sales enablement at some of the most successful and innovative companies in the world, including Siebel Systems (acquired by Oracle), NetApp, Business Objects (acquired by SAP), 3PAR (acquired by HP), PayPal, Salesforce.com, Oracle Marketing Cloud, and Marketo. Working with these companies was an amazing ride, but this was just chapter one of my life's story. I later collaborated with some of the brightest minds in sales enablement to launch a boutique sales enablement and sales coaching firm, Roderick Jefferson and Associates.

My firm has partnered with some of the most innovative companies globally and utilizes cutting-edge technologies designed to accelerate speed-to-revenue, increase sales productivity, and deploy scalable reinforcement strategies. We have a stellar combination of the most experienced people in the business and the most trusted solutions in the marketplace.

In this book, I will share tips, best practices, personal examples, and stories that will provide you with the blueprint required to navigate the twists and turns of becoming a sales enablement practitioner. This blueprint will ultimately empower you to design, deploy, measure, and iterate the types of programs that will lead to success and respect within your field.

Regardless of where your company is in its maturation cycle, the ultimate purpose of sales enablement is to partner with sales leaders to build and execute on strategies that decrease ramp-up (time to revenue) and increase productivity—which all ultimately leads to increased revenue. Remember, enablement is a team effort. We do not drive revenue, but when done correctly, we can certainly make a strong case for how we influence it. I do not believe that sales enablement is what keeps a company's doors open, but I can guarantee that lack of strategic, long-term, consistent, and repeatable enablement will lead to the doors closing.

At its core, the practice of sales enablement is based on a mutually equitable relationship rooted in the desire to help the company mature, grow, and be successful. This is truly where the science of sales enablement meets the art of change management. I hope that you enjoy reading this book as much as I enjoyed crafting this amazing ride that we now call *Sales Enablement 3.0!*

Now let's get started on our journey together.

#HopeIsNotAStrategy

PART I: The Rise of Sales Enablement 3.0

Chapter 1

WHAT DOES SALES ENABLEMENT REALLY DO?

Sales enablement is top-of-mind for a lot of C-level leaders these days, but the problem with sales enablement is that if you ask 10 people what it is, you will likely get 10 different answers. We're still circling around to a globally accepted definition. Some say it's defined as onboarding new employees with a focus on building a solid foundational experience that leads to long-term success. Others say that it's all about providing sales professionals with tools, templates, and processes. Some will say it's about doing whatever it takes to ensure that a company's messaging and positioning is deployed consistently to prospects and customers.

None of these answers are wrong, yet none of them show the full picture. I would venture to say that sales enablement is a combination of all of these components, which is why such an apparently simple question is so complicated.

In its purest form, sales enablement is a thrilling up-and-down roller coaster ride that influences increased revenue. It drives sales teams to peak performance and customers to brand loyalty. The philosophy that binds all aspects of sales enablement is the belief that scalable and repeatable practices lead to increased revenue. Sales enablement is therefore centered around getting sales teams into the right conversations with the right decision makers at the right time, and all in the right way.

Sales enablement has a broad and powerful impact on business success, which means that it's no longer just an option for a business but is now a necessity. Enablement is not a break-fix situation or a simple sales training solution, but instead a delicate balance of building and deploying a tools-based ecosystem designed to prepare our sales professionals to approach prospects and customers differently, while simultaneously removing non-revenue generating activities from their daily lives.

Above all else, sales enablement is NOT about short-term solutions to long-term problems. If you understand this important truth, then you're already halfway to understanding what Sales Enablement 3.0 is all about!

Sales Enablement: It's Not Just Training

Years ago I learned what happens when a company focuses too exclusively on training. I had accepted the position of director of sales enablement at Jigsaw, which at the time was a six-year-old hypergrowth company. Because the company had done so well with selling their product and services, training was viewed as the fix or answer to all problems. If sales leaders said they needed more pipeline, they threw training at it. If there was a problem with discovery and qualification early in the sales cycle, they threw training at it. And if sales professionals were not meeting quota because they couldn't address customer objections? Again, you guessed it, the answer was to throw training at it.

My initial strategy was to perform an assessment with the goal of understanding what the root causes or symptoms were, versus trying to fix what may or may not actually be broken. First, I met with the sales leaders to get their perspectives. Interestingly, each had different reasons or justifications for how they got there and why they should continue to do things the way they had always been done. I also met with the sales professionals to get their perspectives. The key was to ask them the same set of questions I had asked the sales leaders previously. This assessment approach gave me an opportunity to see where there were connections and disconnections between the goals of the sales leaders and what was being done in the field by sales professionals.

It didn't take long to figure out that the biggest disconnect wasn't the process or approach, but rather how the processes were communicated and inconsistently modeled by the sales leaders. Each leader had their own way of onboarding, forecasting, sales performance management, etc. This was creating so much confusion and frustration for the sales professionals that they began creating their own messaging, positioning, and processes, all of which led to a need for repetitive training in an effort to fix the same problems over and over again.

Once the root cause was found, the solution became glaringly apparent: I needed to work with each of the sales leaders to harness their best practices and streamline them into a flexible framework or playbook. This strategy would help to alleviate the confusion and frustration on the part of the sales professionals, and would also drive accountability with the sales leaders by building consistent and repeatable programs based upon their best practices.

In essence, I was using the sales leaders' own ideas and converting them into scalable best practices. The new approach was exactly what they had asked for, so it was now harder for them to not adopt and model the processes that would meet the agreed-upon definition of success.

The final step was to add revenue-impacting metrics and measurements. I went back to the sales leaders with examples of how my sales enablement organization was impacting revenue while simultaneously creating alignment between the sales leaders and sales professionals. The biggest improvements, I explained, can come from the smallest of adjustments if you can get everyone to own their part of the process. The key to success is to focus on *why*, not just *how*, this would create long-term success through collaboration. This is how sales enablement can migrate from being viewed as a training or problem-fixing organization to being a valued sales partner.

It is time to shift our mindset away from the old premise of training. Training is a single, one-time event with little to no reinforcement. While training is a component of enablement, it is just one of many components. Enablement is an ongoing occurrence that must be engrained into the fabric of a company's goals, deliverables, and culture in order to be successful.

Don't get me wrong, training is a critical component, and when done correctly it contributes to success. But training is **NOT** the answer to all problems and should **NEVER** be the first response given. As sales enablement practitioners, we transform training from a single event—whether a boot camp, workshop, or certification—into an ongoing occurrence by aligning these events into role-specific Guided Learning Paths (GLPs) that allow for a continuous learning experience.

Asking Questions, Having Conversations, Creating Long-Term Growth

If you've been in the sales enablement space for a while, you probably know about the one question that you must be prepared to answer. While it seems like a relatively easy question, I'd caution you to stop, breathe, and formulate a clear, concise, and consistent answer. Not to sound overly dramatic, but it could be the make-or-break moment that will either propel or kill your sales enablement career. Now without further ado, here is the all-important question:

What **EXACTLY** does sales enablement **DO**?

I remember the first time a senior executive asked me this. I was working for Siebel Systems, which at the time was the hottest Customer Relationship Management (CRM) company in Silicon Valley. The question came directly from the CEO, Tom Siebel. I was so stunned that I replied with the old tried and true answer of "that's a really good question," which we all know is code for "I don't have an answer that will make me sound credible so let me get back to you." That was the beginning of my attempt at figuring out my answer—and it turned out that the answer kept evolving over the past 20+ years, as sales enablement has grown and matured.

I have come to understand that the goal of sales enablement is to build longstanding, mutually equitable relationships that will lead to the maturation, growth, and success of the company. The specifics and processes will depend on the company itself, but the overarching goal is to imbed durable tools and processes that will ensure the company's success over the long term.

How exactly is this implemented? There are so many tools and techniques in the sales enablement toolbox, but here are six of the most important components for any sales enablement practitioner, change management agent, and orchestrator of all things good in the universe. (Okay, I added that last part, but you have to admit that it sounds impressive and cool!)

1. Decrease new hire ramp-up time

2. Increase operational productivity and efficiency

3. Orchestrate change and growth, whether with local, national, international, new leadership, acquisition, etc.

4. Provide scalable, consistent tools and processes across the lifecycle of a sale

5. Be a change management agent who drives increased incremental revenue

6. Use metrics, tracking, and reporting to substantiate return on investment (ROI)

I have learned over the years that asking questions and having conversations are two of the best ways to ensure the success of any sales enablement program. When I began my career in sales training, I decided to allow my key internal customers—who happened to be sales leadership—to tell me what *they* believed the solution was. They wanted to create stronger sales professionals by removing selling obstacles, many of them said.

Although this wasn't called sales enablement at the time, this is actually what they were asking for. They wanted me to build a group of champions, without realizing that this task simultaneously would achieve the longer-term goals of creating longstanding, mutually equitable relationships that lead to the maturation, growth, and success of the company.

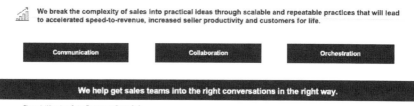

We break the complexity of sales into practical ideas through scalable and repeatable practices that will lead to accelerated speed-to-revenue, increased seller productivity and customers for life.

| Communication | Collaboration | Orchestration |

We help get sales teams into the right conversations in the right way.

Figure 1: What does Sales Enablement Really Do?

With this premise in mind, it is important to remember that the definition, roles, responsibilities, goals, and deliverables of a sales enablement organization will continually shift based upon the maturation cycle and needs of a company. This tends to create a level of confusion around the boundaries of the sales enablement organization. It is therefore important to share what sales enablement is **NOT**!

1. Sales Enablement is **NOT** a one-size-fits-all solution.
    The needs of the business will determine what sales
    enablement means in your company. In some companies
    it is defined as onboarding, while in others it includes
    processes, platforms, and programs. In other companies it
    may also include alliance and partner enablement.

2. Sales Enablement is **NOT** the answer to every question.
    Just because something isn't working well within a
    company doesn't mean that sales enablement is the magic
    answer. My recommendation is to begin your strategy
    by diagnosing the reasons behind the problem before
    serving up sales enablement as the solution.

3. Sales Enablement is **NOT** just training. As I mentioned
    earlier, training is one of the components of sales
    enablement, but it is not the definition. Training without
    a sustainable continuing education process is oftentimes
    worse than not addressing the problem at all because it
    becomes another selling obstacle that takes away from

revenue-generating activities. How many times have you heard, *Our new hires are taking too long to ramp up*, or, *How do we scale the successful habits of top performers?* The appropriate answer is rarely that we only need more training!

4. Sales Enablement is **NOT** information technology (IT). This just means that sales enablement should not be the *break-fix* organization that companies only think about when something is broken.

If your company, CEO, or top sales leadership executive views sales enablement as a *break-fix* solution, then I recommend working quickly to show the value of your programs in order to change their perspective. You need to work diligently to show that your value is more than simply building training programs or sharing vanity statistics workshops. If you're not able to change their perspective, then you're destined to fail in your role.

Given that sales enablement is about much more than fixing short-term problems, the two most important skills needed as a sales enablement practitioner are *listening* and *asking the right questions*. Without these skills, it's impossible to dig deeper and discover the company's true needs.

I remember the first time I learned this lesson. It was my first day of new hire sales training at AT&T—and at the time, their approach to training was considered groundbreaking. I was part of a group of first-time sales professionals sent to New Jersey (AT&T headquarters) for a six-week-long training program. It was an experiential, hands-on workshop that aligned to the lifecycle of a sale and ended with a group-based presentation requiring each team member to stand and deliver the AT&T sales pitch based upon specific buyer personas.

I remember walking into a brightly lit training room with no windows and about a dozen tables arranged in working pods. The sales trainer greeted each of us as we found our names on the tent cards and met our working groups. Once seated, we noticed easels situated next to each table covered with colored markers, candy, and toys. With a bit of apprehension and a lot of curiosity, the training began.

The first words out of the trainer's mouth would forever shape my view of sales. She said, "Look to your left and to your right. Less than 50 percent of the people in this room will experience a successful sales career."

While it seemed callous at the time, based upon my experience, she could not have been more accurate. She then approached me with a question that would alter my approach to sales. She looked me squarely in the face and said, "If you needed to eat and only had this pen to sell, how would you sell it to me?"

As with most of the room's participants, I immediately began to talk about the features and benefits of the pen, only to be continually challenged with the words *go deeper*. Every time she said this, I took it as a personal challenge to impress her with my knowledge of fountain pens. This went on for what felt like hours, although I'm sure it was no more than five minutes. At that point she finally said the word that I needed to hear: *Sold!*

I watched as she repeated this process over and over, as each participant struggled to make the sale. At the end of the exercise, the woman explained that it took us so long to close because we were attempting to sell features of the pen without confirming what was important to the buyer. We were talking, but we weren't asking the right questions. Her exercise highlighted the importance of discovery and qualification by asking questions rather than spewing facts, figures, features, and benefits.

The number one question that every sales enablement professional should ask when approaching a new company initiative or program is: *What business problem are we trying to solve?* This will prevent you from being distracted by the noise that might veer you away from your goals and deliverables.

It's easy to understand why the importance of *asking questions* has been difficult for many sales professionals to learn. It wasn't so long ago that asking questions wasn't such an important part of the sales process. In order to understand how we got to where we are today, let's take a look back at the history of sales and sales enablement.

Chapter 2:

A BRIEF HISTORY OF SALES ENABLEMENT

WE ARE HERE TO CREATE HISTORY, NOT REPEAT IT.
—*Chantelle Renee*

With all of the growing hype surrounding sales enablement, it's easy to believe that the concept is new and innovative. While that is half accurate—in that sales enablement is constantly coming up with new and innovative tools—the truth is that it has been around for a very long time. But it wasn't always called sales enablement.

The essence of sales "enablement," as per its name, is simply the processes, tools, and philosophies that *enable* selling. These tools and processes have, of course, changed significantly over the years. With that in mind, I like to divide the history of sales enablement into three distinct eras—sales enablement 1.0, sales enablement 2.0, and sales enablement 3.0.

Sales enablement 1.0 was the era of the traveling salesperson, when sales was a one-time transaction based on the salesperson convincing the client that they needed the product. While this era is now long gone, the attitudes from that time still influence sales, especially the focus on convincing the costumer about a one-time purchase. As we will see, this orientation can be harmful in today's 3.0 era.

Sales enablement 2.0 spanned several decades. This is the time period that most of today's salespeople grew up with. Enablement 2.0 was the era of improved digital technologies, when selling became dominated by data and analytics. In some ways, the 2.0 era is still dominant, but it's now in the process of being replaced with *Sales Enablement 3.0*, which more fully embraces the buyer and their journey. Indeed, the evolution of the buyer's journey has been the foundational shift that led to the 3.0 era.

From One-Time Transactions to the Buyer's Journey

The buying process has changed significantly over the past several years. According to the Content Marketing Institute, "62% of B2B buyers say they can make a business decision based on online content alone." Buyers are now far savvier and further along in the buying process before engaging with sales professionals. The Institute also noted that 80% of B2B buyers will view at least five pieces of content during the buying process, and half of them will view more than eight pieces.

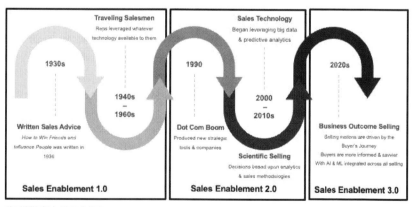

Figure 2. The History of Sales Enablement

While the sales enablement 1.0 and 2.0 eras served their purpose during each of its periods, they have fallen short or are no longer relevant in today's world. There is no back to normal, no return to the way we used to sell. It is now all about defining the *next normal* for your people and processes. Yet in order to understand and embrace the new normal, it's important to know what once was, and why these past circumstances have changed. Let's dig a little deeper into the previous eras.

SALES ENABLEMENT 1.0: Let's travel back to the 1930s. During this time period and moving all the way forward into the 1970s and '80s, selling was focused on how to message and position the Return on Investment (ROI) for all goods and services. This was an intrinsic trait, so it led to the first iteration of what would become sales training, a one-time event that would ultimately lead to an exchange of goods or services at a negotiated cost. The techniques behind sales training and the power of persuasion were epitomized in Dale Carnegie's 1936 landmark book, *How to Win Friends and Influence People*.

The 1940s-1960s brought us the traveling salespeople who utilized whatever technology was available to them to close the deal. This applied to everything from snake oil salespeople to heavy machinery and equipment sales to household utilities to items as basic as kitchen cutlery. They all had one thing in common: They wanted to convince their customers that a particular tool or service, once purchased, would cause their lives to be enhanced and enriched in ways that they had never thought imaginable.

You guessed it, sales at that time was all about convincing people that the salesperson had something that they couldn't live without, or better yet that they would be left behind their friends and family members if they did not purchase it. Once the convincing was done, all that was left was the one-time transaction. This served companies and the overall national economy well by creating revenue from selling never-before-seen products and services that may or may not actually work as promised.

I'm pretty sure that this is where the phrase *never confuse marketing and sales* was coined! Now that the foundation for a consumer- and sales-based economy was in place, there were seemingly endless opportunities to sell on a level never before imagined. Dare I say that a monster had been created, and it could not be put back into the proverbial box.

SALES ENABLEMENT 2.0: For half a century, sales continued to be based on practices first developed in the 1930s. The huge leap occurred in the 1990s, when the "dot com" boom introduced new, innovative, and scalable tools that companies leveraged for sales growth. With this shift we had officially moved into sales enablement 2.0, where scale and automation were used to make sales professionals more effective, efficient, and productive.

This created a fundamental shift from focusing primarily on ROI to selling based upon perceived or contrived pain. Let's just call it **FEAR, UNCERTAINTY, and DOUBT (FUD).** This change shook the business world to its core and would change the way that business would be done forever. We were in a time of indulgence, meaning that everything had to be bigger, faster, and stronger, and innovation was a must-have.

I remember working at AT&T when we began selling a service called AT&T WorldNet, which was basic dial-up internet access. (Yes, there was a time when the internet was not readily available to the general public and was actually accessed via a telephone line.) Most companies were skeptical of this new technology. This is where the true sales skills came in of convincing prospects that not only did they *need* the service, but they could risk losing market share and their competitive advantage if they did not purchase it.

This was the shift from focusing on ROI to also considering the Cost of Inaction (COI), meaning what your business would miss out on by not purchasing the product. This shift was responsible for a fundamental change in how sales moved forward. Before this time, it was about showing business value, meaning that all of the cool bells and whistles all ultimately helped your business either increase productivity and efficiency or decrease pain. But now there was this all-important third factor, i.e., the COI.

The 2.0 era was all about the accelerating importance of scale, automation, and analytics. These all continue to inform the 3.0 era, so let's take a closer look at how analytics and big data foundationally changed sales.

The Impact of Scale, Automation, and Analytics

The late 1990s through early 2000s was all about scale and automation. The creation of Sales Force Automation software (SFA) by Siebel Systems, which migrated into Customer Relationship Management (CRM) solutions, was another game-changer. Now, spreadsheets were deemed passé because companies could maintain all of their customer contact, sales calendar, opportunity, and forecasting information in a single location. These platforms required a different level of training in order to maximize such expensive tools. Training shifted from one-to-one interactions to one-to-many presentations with the inception of eLearning tools and individualized recording tools that could add voice and video to a basic PowerPoint presentation.

Sales technology took a huge leap in the 2000s when companies began to leverage big data analytics. The year 2010 to present has been very focused on analytics. This created a shift from positioning around the Cost of Inaction (COI) to focusing on scientific selling. What this meant was that customers were equipped with richer, more actionable information on a level that we had never experienced before. It also meant that they were usually further into the sales cycle before they met with a sales professional to receive the traditional, canned product demo before making a purchasing decision. The ability to bypass a sales professional and buy via a self-service model began to alter the interaction between buyer and seller.

This was the beginning of the pivotal, monumental change from training being seen as a single event to the development of sales enablement 3.0. This is an ongoing occurrence of events tied to metrics and reinforcement activities. It has been a true paradigm shift for companies.

For some people and companies, the shift from the 2.0 to 3.0 mindset has been slow. The focus on metrics and analytics rather than the buyer's journey has enticed sales enablement practitioners to get too comfortable with our widely accepted processes, programs, and basic rudimentary tools. We stick with the old, comfortable procedures, such as using voiceover PowerPoint, to deliver messaging and Excel spreadsheets to track participant registration, engagement, and task completions. Too many sales enablement organizations are viewed solely as trainers, without being able to substantiate a hardline return on investment to the company.

While I have seen tremendous advancement in technology and platforms during my years as a sales enablement practitioner, I cannot say the same for the sales enablement profession in general. As the buyer's journey, competitive landscape, and selling motions continue to evolve, too much of sales enablement seems to have gotten stuck in a time warp. But what if sales enablement stopped being perceived as a cost center? What if, instead of thinking of sales enablement as training, onboarding, or the resting place for an organization's broken things, we thought of sales enablement as a strategic investment? What if sales enablement was viewed as a proactive function that actually enables salespeople to sell more, sell higher, and sell faster?

How do we move from being viewed as the *fixers of broken things* to being appreciated as valued business partners across the company? Well, that is the basic premise of sales enablement 3.0. It will require yet another fundamental shift in how we enable sales professionals to help prospects and customers instead of simply selling to them.

Within the sales enablement 3.0 mindset, it is clear that just because someone is in a sales role doesn't mean they should always be selling. The baseline of sales is asking the right questions, clarifying what you heard, then finding the correct solutions to address the prospect's problems or pain. This means that it is time to *stop giving presentations and start having conversations!* In order to be effective, this must be driven by the sales enablement organization in partnership with the sales leadership team. If you are still enabling sales professionals to focus on selling products, services, or even solutions, then you are doing them, your company, your prospect, and your customers a disservice.

While the previous sales enablement time periods served us well for many years, it is now time to take sales enablement to the next level. It is time to welcome the shift to sales enablement 3.0.

Chapter 3

WELCOME TO
SALES ENABLEMENT 3.0!

**THERE'S NO SHORTAGE OF REMARKABLE IDEAS, WHAT'S MISSING IS A
WILL TO EXECUTE THEM.**

—Seth Godin

The shift into sales enablement 3.0 will require a foundational change from focusing on sales productivity alone to increasing communication and relationships. You may be wondering, *Why can't we just stay in our comfort zone?* Well, the answer is quite simple. If we keep doing things the way we have always done things, we will continue to degrade the value of sales enablement and be relegated, in some cases, to being viewed as sales scribes, sales servants, and even worse, *the fixers of broken things*!

The time has come to fully focus on *business outcome conversations*. It is time to adjust the discovery and qualification process by asking, listening, and hearing rather than simply asking questions to get the answers that sales professionals need to move the sale forward. It is time for *you*, as a sales enablement practitioner, to get comfortable with being uncomfortable! This is the only way to change the way that you assess, build, communicate, deploy, measure, reinforce, and iterate your programs.

21

As mentioned in the previous chapter, the 3.0 era was ushered in by big changes in the buyer's journey. These days, buyers often initiate conversations with salespeople after they have done a lot of research on their own. This means that salespeople must focus more on the buyer's journey, how decisions are made, by whom, and when services are purchased instead of focusing mostly on sales, processes, stages, and tools.

It is no longer enough to have a single person responsible for training. This now requires role-specific, business–acumen sales enablement practitioners who are responsible for sales professionals as well as sales managers. A related development is the new importance of the Software as a Service (SaaS) model. This is a method of software delivery that allows data to be accessed from any device with an internet connection and web browser. In this web-based model, software vendors host and maintain the servers, the databases, and the code that make up an application.

These new models mean that sales professionals must simultaneously adjust to the changes in the buyer's journey *and* this new way of showing the key differentiation, competitive advantage, and business value of their solutions and services. This has been a significant challenge for sales enablement practitioners because we can no longer rely on training people in the way we used to.

It's now more important than ever to get closer to prospects and to understand their needs, goals, and deliverables. We also now work closer than ever with the internal lines of business to ensure that we are delivering clear, concise, and consistent messaging both internally and externally.

Sales enablement organizations are changing the types of people, skillsets, and roles needed to thrive. The way that we communicate metrics around sales performance—along with the platforms we use to scale and automate our sales enablement activities—are shifting. The end result is that marketing, product marketing, product management, sales operations, human resources, professional services, customer success, customer support, and sales enablement are becoming a more collaborative team, with less emphasis on the processes and methodologies that had previously put these sectors at odds with one another.

In today's competitive environment, the focus for many companies has shifted to the customer. This means that deliverables have also shifted. The validation points are now about helping our customers to increase profitability, reduce cost, and mitigate risk. These are the baseline metrics that are crucial for the survival, growth, and success of a company in today's economy.

Changes in Buying Cycles and Decision Criteria

As sales enablement practitioners, we often complain that senior leaders don't understand the importance of our craft and don't appreciate the value that we add. In many cases, the fault for this lack of understanding and appreciation lies with us. We don't speak the language of business, and we don't always do a good job of strategically aligning our programs to their goals. We don't always communicate effectively up-front to describe the planned impact, agree upon roles, and define responsibilities. Finally, we do not clearly enough tie our value to metrics around increasing incremental revenue.

Want to know how to move from being viewed as simply training to being valued as a true business partner? You must have a clear, concise strategy in place that defines every component related to the end-to-end process of sales enablement, and it must all be articulated in your internal customer's language. And the easiest way to understand a company's goals and desired deliverables is to embrace the new core realties of the Sales Enablement 3.0 era. These include changes in buying cycles—as mentioned before—as well as shifts in decision criteria for companies and level of access to the C-suite. Let's look at each of these more closely.

Extended Buying Cycles, More Decision Makers:

According to the *Harvard Business Review*, "The number of people involved in B2B solution purchases has climbed from an average of 5.4 two years ago to 6.8 today, and these internal customers come from a lengthening roster of roles, functions, and geographies... the increase in the number of individuals in the buying process has added an additional level of complexity to the process." As sales enablement practitioners, the onus is on us to accommodate and adapt to these huge changes in the internal buying process. I learned this lesson myself the hard way.

I was working with a marketing automation company that was purchasing a new Learning Management System (LMS) to replace their old, antiquated system. I worked with what I believed to be every line of business that would be leveraging the tool. This meant collaborating with sales, marketing, information technology, and professional services to ensure that all of their success criteria were included in the Request for Proposal (RFP) before it was crafted and deployed to our top three vendors.

This wasn't my first time driving this type of process, so I felt like all voices were heard, all selection criteria were included, and all boxes were checked. This assumption is why things got really ugly.

Word quickly spread across the company that they were selecting a final vendor to own the implementation and training around the new LMS. Before I knew it, I was approached by our head of channels and alliances as well as our head of Learning & Development with requests to be included in the project. What had seemed like a well-coordinated project now needed to include additional lines of business. This meant more communication updates, more meeting participants, and more success criteria, all of which now needed to be included in the RFP before the selection processes could be finalized. Not only did this increase the amount of work required to complete and submit the RFP, but it extended the project kickoff, deliverables timeframes, and completion date of the project.

I learned a very valuable lesson from this project: always build additional time into your project plan in preparation for what *could* go wrong. It's better to prepare for exceptions and not need them than to incur one and not be prepared for them.

In a more general sense, this experience also deepened my understanding of changes to the internal decision-making process. In the sales enablement 3.0 era, sales professionals must successfully articulate value to a larger number of decision makers, and they must do this across multiple disciplines so that it resonates with each of them, individually. Sales enablement must prepare sales professionals to speak the language of their buyers. It all begins with understanding the goals and deliverables of each buyer, then speaking directly to each of them at the proper level. For example, when speaking to a CFO, it's critical to focus on mitigating risk and cutting cost. This emphasis, however, may not resonate when meeting with the VP of Sales, because their focus is on accelerating speed-to-revenue and increasing seller productivity.

This increase in the number of individuals in the buying process has also led to an extension in payment terms. According to Chorus.ai, "Payment terms longer than 30 days have doubled since the beginning of March 2020." How can you impact this extended buying cycle? It all begins with getting the right people in the right conversation, at the right level, with the right tools and assets. While this may sound complex and difficult, it is actually the baseline of what we do as sales enablement practitioners. The difficult part of this equation is finding a balance between the right level of enablement and allowing your sales professionals to do what they do best, which is to interact with prospects and customers in order to drive increased revenue.

Decision Criteria for Companies Has Shifted: In the 3.0 era, more decision makers are involved, and the criteria that they consider when buying has changed as well. More than ever, companies are putting a stronger emphasis on reducing costs and mitigating risks above the traditional focus on increasing sales volume when making buying decisions.

There was a time when the definition of success for sales enablement practitioners was based upon three key metrics:

- Decreasing time to revenue (accelerating movement through the sales funnel)

- Increasing sales productivity (continuing education, coaching, and reinforcement)

- Deploying strategy, architecture, and execution (processes, programs, and platforms)

These metrics are still important, but they're no longer the sole measurements of success for a sales enablement organization. Due to global economic changes, natural disasters, and medical crises, there has been a shift in how sellers buy. These changes, in turn, will necessitate change in how sales enablement practitioners prepare sales professionals to sell. In addition to the above criteria, these days sales enablement practitioners must enhance their focus on the following:

- Business Outcome Selling: Shifting from volume velocity (features, benefits, products) selling to a focus on key differentiation, competitive advantage, and the business value of buying from your company.

- Increasing Profits: Articulating how buying from your company will directly impact the financial health of their company.

- Mitigating Risk: This is critical. It is important that sales professionals include both companywide and personal reasons to buy from your company.

Sales enablement practitioners will need to discontinue the traditional approach of focusing solely on ROI. We must now include the Cost of Inaction (COI) in the sales position. COI in its purest form means, "What happens if your company doesn't buy from my company? Will you lose your competitive edge? Will you potentially miss out on an increased revenue stream? Will you miss an opportunity around market expansion? Will you lose credibility with your buyers by not appearing to be innovative or cutting edge?"

Keep in mind that COI is *not* to be used as a scare tactic, but an opportunity to have a quantifiable conversation around how not buying could lead to losing market share. There are a number of factors such as losing a competitive edge, a lag in innovation, or the inability to prepare their sales professionals for the unknown obstacles that the ever-changing business landscape may bring.

The C-suite is far more accessible than ever before: According to Chorus.ai, in the year 2020 there was "a 45% increase of sales leaders joining meetings compared to 2019, and a 36%

increase of leaders from the buying-side participating in sales conversations." These days, there is an enormous amount of pressure placed on sales leaders to meet or exceed quota. Not hitting quota in 2-3 consecutive quarters can cost a sales leader his or her job. For this reason, executives—especially sales leaders—are now more intimately involved in every complex sales cycle to ensure that their teams have been given every opportunity to win deals. Expect the vice president of Sales or the chief revenue officer to be intimately involved in all deals. Now more than ever, each of their purchases are not only being scrutinized, but can even impact their careers.

With this increased level of access to the C-suite comes a deeper level of sales enablement required. Sales professionals are looking to sales enablement to ensure that they are prepared to speak to each of your company's buying personas, in their language, with a focus on what is top of mind to each of them. You may need to get a bit more granular when it comes to ensuring that their discovery and qualification skills are polished, preparing them to handle a complex level of objections, and helping them understand not only what is top of mind for leaders, but how to articulate the value of your products and services in a clear, concise, and consistent manner.

The Four Key Components: Focus, Unite, Adjust, Incorporate

Now that we understand some of the changes that must be embraced in the 3.0 era, let's turn to building a thriving sales enablement organization!

Do you have the right kind of IEP (Ideal Employee Profile) in place? Are you taking advantage of the available talent pool to enhance your sales teams? How will you enable your sales teams to clearly, concisely, and consistently message, position, and sell differently in this new era? Are you coaching your sales leaders to lead with empathy, humanity, and Emotional Intelligence (EQ) on a deeper level than ever before?

Today, sales professionals and leaders are looking to sales enablement practitioners for creative, actionable, relationship-driven ways to advance and close deals. This is where sales enablement must be prepared, as a business partner, to enable in a very different way than we ever have done before.

I believe that there are four key components to designing, building, and deploying the shift to sales enablement 3.0. These components are focus, unite, adjust, and incorporate.

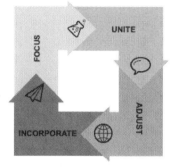

Focus your energy, goals and deliverables on things that you can impact and that will align with your company's goals. *Everything else is just noise!*

Commit to designing, building and incorporating an innovative customer experience into your go-to-market strategy in order to delineate your company as the clear thought leader in your space.

Relationships are the backbone of success. There has never been a time where leading with humanity, empathy, and emotional intelligence has meant more than today.

Pivot to delivering deeper value around improving discovery skills, increasing profits, reducing costs, risk mitigation, and facilitating business outcome selling conversations.

Figure 3: Sales Enablement 3.0 Framework

1. **Focus:** This is all about getting rid of the noise! You must remove any exterior, non-revenue generating activities from your sales enablement programs. Instead, focus your energy, activities, goals, deliverables, and resources on things that you can impact. These must all be directly aligned with your company's goals.

   Your company is counting on you to wade through the noise and provide programs, processes, tools, and platforms that will drive accelerated speed-to-revenue and increased sales productivity and efficiency, all while helping the customer success organization to create satisfied customers for life. Along these lines, a successful sales enablement organization must create connection points so that the front-of-house (sales) is tightly connected and collaborating with the back-of-house (customer success and customer support). The goal is to create a clear, concise, and consistent customer experience beginning with the initial qualification conversation all the way across the customer's lifecycle.

2. **Unite:** In the 3.0 era, relationships are the backbone of
    success. There has never been a time where leading with
    humanity, empathy, and emotional intelligence has meant
    more than it does today. It is no longer enough to simply
    say that you care about your prospects and customers
    in your marketing materials. Now you have to show
    it in every interaction, outbound communication, and
    conversation.

    In the past, businesses owned their brand and how it was
    viewed. The uptake of globally available social media
    has forever shifted that into the hands of your prospects
    and customers. This doesn't mean that companies don't
    have some control, but the level of control has definitely
    changed. We now have entire organizations responsible
    for reacting to customer issues via every social media
    platform available. All it takes is one negative review to
    change how a company and its services are perceived.
    There is nothing more precious today than a happy, satis-
    fied, digitally savvy customer!

3. **Adjust:** This simply means that a sales enablement
    3.0 organization must fully adjust to change! All
    conversations are now focused on the experience of
    partnering with your company and its business outcomes.
    The days of selling features, benefits, and solutions are
    long gone. Instead, *adjust* to delivering a customer-
    focused approach. This means improving discovery skills,
    mapping the buyer's journey, increasing profits, reducing
    costs, mitigating risk, and facilitating business outcome
    selling conversations with a focus on helping your
    customers retain their existing customers.

    Adjusting also means preparing your sales professionals
    to interact with prospects in meaningful ways that lead
    to a lasting relationship with your company. Your sales
    professionals must be armed with all of the messaging,

positioning, and objection-handling strategies required to feel competent and confident. This includes mapping out the buyer's landscape and enabling your sales professionals to identify and address the compelling events, questions, timing, and buying committees that will drive the advancement toward a closed sale. This is a critical component that many companies leave out of the enablement process. Too often, companies are focused on fitting the customer into their selling motions rather than taking time to map out the buyer's journey and landscape. We will closely examine the buyer's journey in chapter 6.

4. **Incorporate:** Any successful sales enablement organization must fully *incorporate* a state-of-the-art sales enablement 3.0 strategy into its go-to-market strategy. This must occur not only as a key differentiator internally, but as an element of your company's external go-to-market strategy as a way of confirming that your company is the clear thought leader in your industry.

In order to implement this strategy, companies will need to design, build, and use content designed to renew and advance conversations with prospects on a level never before thought of. It's no longer about simply being customer focused. The adoption and implementation of the Sales Enablement 3.0 strategy will require a change of mindset, skillsets, and communication skills to become customer-centric. This means that every conversation, tool, process, platform, and deliverable must be focused on increasing productivity and efficiency or decreasing pain for the customer.

Even companies that have the *intent* of adopting a new strategy often struggle to implement it. Sometimes this is because of a lack of will; sometimes the problem is a lack of knowledge. With that in mind, let's strengthen your knowledge base with a step-by-step recipe for designing, building, and implementing a world-class sales enablement organization.

Chapter 4

CRAFTING THE SALES ENABLEMENT 3.0 BLUEPRINT

SALES ENABLEMENT IS BOTH AN ART AND A SCIENCE. THE PROCESS IS LIKE A SWAN; ALL YOU SEE IS THE GRACEFUL GLIDE ACROSS THE WATER, BUT UNDERNEATH IS WHERE THE WORK IS REALLY HAPPENING.

~ Roderick Jefferson

Now that we understand the importance of shifting to a 3.0 mindset, it's time to dig deeper and get to the fun part—assembling your team and crafting your road map to success! As with any organization, the first and most important ingredient is the people who make it up.

I have found that most sales enablement teams have been created based upon a sense of overwhelming need. Generally, companies outgrow the ability for sales leaders to focus on leading, coaching, and training their sales teams. This leads to either promoting one of the company's best sales professionals—which can create new problems—or hiring the company's first sales enablement practitioner.

Given all of the uncertainty in the world today, the traditional hiring and placement processes have been uprooted. Employees now have a higher need to feel safe. We are experiencing unprecedented access to seasoned, successful sales professionals who are also unemployed. There is an opportunity here, and companies are reevaluating the definition of their Ideal Employee Profile (IEP), which we'll explore more later.

Assembling the Sales Enablement Team

The key functions that make up a sales enablement organization will depend on the size of your company as well as the maturation point of your company. In general, the roles and responsibilities will include leaders, program managers, trainers, instructional designers, and coordinators.

Figure 4: Building a World Class Sales Enablement Organization

Sales Enablement Leader. This is typically a seasoned vice president, senior director, or director. This person is responsible for setting the organization's scope and vision, designing and leading with strategic focus on the design, development, implementation tools, programs, processes, and metrics. They are also the voice of the customer and the field within the company's leadership team.

Program Managers. These individuals should be viewed as an extension of the sales segment or regional leader that they support. They're responsible for sales leadership engagement, identifying skill gaps, sharing best practices, and driving two-way communication with the sales leader.

Trainers. These individuals are responsible for building specific training programs and preparing teaching plans, as well as developing or overseeing the production of classroom materials and facilitation.

Instructional Designers. These individuals are responsible for curriculum design, development, and updates. They should also be responsible for identifying the appropriate delivery modalities, which include audio, video, podcasts, simulations, role plays, gamification, etc.

Shared Resources. These individuals are responsible for the coordination of program logistics, needs analysis and survey updates, deployments, and tabulation, as well as communications, survey scores, metrics, tracking, and reporting. While this is usually an entry-level position, it should not be positioned as a low-level administrative role. When done correctly, I've seen this role used as a migration point into a program manager, trainer, or instructional designer role within the sales enablement team.

As you can see, each of these roles serves a specific function within the sales enablement team. It's not the roles themselves that will drive success, but the level of interdependency and balance of responsibility that is required to meet the needs of the sales organization across the buyer's journey.

I once built a sales enablement team that became the blueprint for all others throughout my career. I was hired as the leader of a soon to be sales enablement organization within one of the most successful and innovative tech companies globally, Oracle Marketing Cloud. Having coached several sports teams, I decided that I would approach this challenge with the same mentality. That meant recruiting, hiring, nurturing, and leading the *right* player for each position on my global team.

This started with program managers who were capable of building relationships and trust with their regional sales leaders. Next came instructional designers who were able to work with the program managers to translate the needs articulated by the sales leaders into consistent and scalable programs, processes, tools, and assets. The next addition to the team were trainers. Their job was to collaborate with the program managers and instructional designers to deliver the content to our sales teams as well as provide feedback around improvements, upgrades, and changes.

The final piece of the team was the linchpin that holds the sales enablement organization together. This is the coordinator. They are the hub that spokes out to every role on the sales enablement team. While they are responsible for logistics, surveys, and metrics tabulation, this is just the tip of the iceberg. They are responsible for scheduling internal and external offsite events as well as driving all communications, not to mention taking on things like impromptu therapy sessions and ensuring that the team stays sane during the best and worst of times.

I had assembled my dream team, and I learned that when I stepped back and allowed them to individually and collectively do what they were hired to do and were passionate about, there was nothing they couldn't accomplish. This team was so innovative, consistent, and successful that they rewrote the definition of what it means to be a world-class sales enablement organization. Their incredible results ultimately led to being named by SiriusDecisions as Sales Enablement Program of the Year in a category that included 250+ global enterprise companies.

The 5 Ps: **Purpose, People, Programs, Performance, Platforms**

As with building a new home, every successful project begins with the end-user in mind. In order to successfully meet the needs of the customer, a blueprint is required so that everyone on the team is aware of the timing as well as their roles and responsibilities. The same applies to crafting the blueprint for success around sales enablement. In this section you will learn the components required to design, deploy, measure, and iterate a successful sales enablement blueprint.

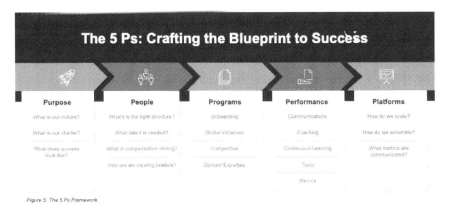

Figure 5: The 5 Ps Framework

Purpose

The first P stands for Purpose. This is like the foundation of a house or basic algebra. It sets the baseline that will lead to the success or failure of the remainder of the process. In order to ensure that your purpose is clearly articulated, the following three key questions must be answered.

- What is our culture?

- What is our charter?

- What does success look like?

People

The Next P stands for People. While each of the 5 Ps has high value, never forget that the most import P stands for people. As a sales enablement practitioner, we are in the *people business.* Our job is to make people bigger, faster, and stronger so that they can close deals faster. In order to ensure that the right people are in place, the following four key questions must be answered:

- What is the organization's structure?

- What type of talent is needed?

- What success criteria will compensation drive?

- Is there a structure in place focused on creating leaders?

Programs

The Next P stands for Programs: There are five key programmatical components that must be designed, built, deployed, and measured. These will vary based upon the needs, growth, and maturation cycle of your company and sales enablement organization.

- Talent Assessment and Acquisition

- Onboarding

- Role Specific Business Acumen

- Sales Leadership Coaching

- Continuing Education and Reinforcement

Performance

The Next P stands for Performance: This is where the *art* meets the *science* of sales enablement. Performance metrics should come from a mix of sources, and communications regarding performance metrics should be shared across your organization. These communications should be of high value to, and in the language of, each of the different internal customers.

There are five key components that must be designed, built, deployed, and measured. Similar to programs, the delivery and timing will vary based upon the needs, growth, and maturation cycle of your company and sales enablement organization.

- Content Management Systems

- Learning Management Systems

- Continuous Learning

- Tools

- Metrics

My recommendation is to collaborate with your business leaders prior to sharing any internal communications regarding performance to ensure that it doesn't get lost in the noise or proverbial mountain of messages being shared across your company. We will focus more on performance in chapter 8.

Platforms

The final P stands for Platforms: I have found that focusing on the tools or platforms that result in accelerated speed-to-revenue, increased seller productivity, and the removal of selling obstacles resonates well with sales leaders. These tools will provide an opportunity for your sales enablement organization to measure and report on metrics that have resulted in an immediate impact on revenue.

Remember, just because a tool or platform is available or successful at another company doesn't mean it will be equally as effective at your company. I highly recommend working with your sales leadership team to determine the short-term, medium-range, and long-term needs of the business. Then allow their needs to be the guiding principle around the tools that will ultimately lead to building your company's sales enablement technology stack. We will be exploring these tools in more detail in chapter 11.

While there are a plethora of sales enablement tools available, there are four key questions that must be answered prior to making a purchase.

- What issues are we addressing?

- Which tools are available to address these issues?

- How will these tools allow your organization to scale and automate tasks?

- What metrics will be communicated to the sales leadership team to validate the value of your organization?

The key to successfully answering these questions is to focus on the outcome of selecting, deploying, and utilizing your sales enablement technology stack. Too many times companies focus on *which* tools they need to enhance their technology stack versus *how* these new tools will make their sales professionals more effective, efficient, and productive.

★

The first time that I successfully implemented my 5 Ps strategy, I was working with a small startup company that was in hyper-growth mode. It had a great set of products but no strategy around how they would build, deploy, and measure a sales enablement technology stack. As with all of my engagements, this one began with an assessment that answered each of the questions outlined above. This process subsequently led to securing the executive support and funding required to enhance the company's sales enablement technology stack.

The first step was determining the nature of the problem. Did the company have skillset issues, which would simply require tools to be deployed through additional training? Or were there scalability issues, which would require a long-term shift in their tools landscape to increase efficiency and productivity? This distinction is critical because it determines not only which type of tools the team needed to research, but more importantly the level of commitment and resources required to successfully complete this engagement.

We determined that the company was facing a scalability issue, and their sales professionals wanted to increase efficiency and productivity through automation. Now that the purpose was squared away, we decided to take two approaches to research. Initially I reached out to a number of sales enablement practitioners in my network via an online survey to get a well-rounded understanding of which tools they were using, what was working well, and what the selection criteria was that led to their ultimate decision to make a purchase.

The second approach was to utilize G2.com, a well-respected online research tool that chooses the right software and services for businesses based on authentic, timely reviews from sales enablement practitioners. Now that we were fully armed with reviews, recommendations, and best practices, we were prepared to move toward the components of a Request for Proposal (RFP) to begin the vendor selection process.

The next step involved the most important P, people, as well as performance. We worked with the sales leadership team to determine what a successful deployment would look like. It was not enough to say that they wanted to increase productivity and efficiency. They needed to implement short-, medium-, and long-term metrics that would validate the cost of the tools and ensure that there was an enablement leader and team in place to successfully implement the technology stack. We agreed to focus on the design and implementation of the tools as short-term goals. We designed a training and enablement plan that included a content review, an upload strategy, and usage metrics. Finally, we agreed to utilize sales metrics such as speed-to-revenue, increased prospect conversations, and increased task completion as long-term metrics.

The final piece of the project was focused on sales leadership communications. Because this engagement was such an integral part of the company's shift in go-to-market strategy, not to mention an expensive endeavor, we decided that initially the sales leadership team would receive weekly updates. These updates would include all milestones, deliverables, best practices, and of course any missteps.
This engagement was successful because we worked collaboratively with the executive and sales leadership teams to define the scope of the project, deeply researched the tools prior to vendor selection, and agreed upon a structured communication plan. We ensured that the sales leadership team was intimately involved in each phase of the engagement so that the outcome was based upon the *needs* of

their sales organization rather than what sales enablement practitioners *thought* they needed.

As the saying goes, "People don't care what you know until they know that you care about what's important to them." Because the sales leadership team was intimately involved in the process, they took ownership of the adoption and execution of the tools, and they ultimately modeled positive behavior of usage for their sales professionals.

I believe that in today's changing business landscape, the delineation between successful companies and unsuccessful ones will be the ability to proactively pivot and make adjustments that will not only meet the new needs of prospects and customers, but actually exceed them in ways never before imagined. This is where the shift to the sales enablement 3.0 strategy comes in. The implementation and execution of this innovative strategy will provide you with an opportunity to show your value as a sales enablement practitioner across your entire company by defining the parameters of what will become the *next* normal.

The old adage has proven again to be true: "One day it is going to rain." These days, it often feels like an absolute storm. The big question is, will you be the one buying the umbrellas, or will you be selling, manufacturing, or even designing them? If you want to be there at the front lines of change, keep reading to learn how to successfully design and implement a world-class sales enablement program.

PART 2:
Deploying a World-Class Sales Enablement Program

Chapter 5

BUILDING THE SALES ENABLEMENT BUSINESS CASE AND CHARTER

*IF THE BUSINESS CASE IS MADE AND THE MONEY IS NEEDED,
THE MONEY WILL BE MADE AVAILABLE*
~ *James Krouse*

N ow that we understand the history, goals, and strategies behind sales enablement 3.0, it's time to put our noses to the proverbial grindstone. Understanding the need for sales enablement is one thing. Implementing the process is quite another! According to the wise words of Ed Ross, CEO of Michigan and Manchester Consulting, "Most businesses know the importance of having a strong sales organization. Despite this, many companies struggle to enable their sales team to perform at a high level."

I remember working with a small high-tech company that was undergoing this shift to sales enablement. The company was growing rapidly, and its sales leaders faced the realization that the level of training required to create efficient and effective sales professionals was taking time away from their ability to lead and coach their sales teams. After a quarter of poor sales results, the chief revenue officer decided to hire the company's first sales enablement leader. This was a step in the right direction, but it created another problem: no one on the sales leadership team had any experience interviewing or hiring a sales enablement practitioner!

This is when they reached out to me to help solve their problem. Through multiple conversations and hours of collaborative, thought-provoking meetings, the sales leadership team realized that this was a pivotal hire in the company's maturation process. There were a number of questions that needed to be answered. How seasoned did the sales enablement leader need to be? What did short- and long-term success look like? How would this person be compensated? Finally, which group or groups of sellers would this person be responsible for enabling?

The end result was that the sales leadership team realized their company had outgrown the need for training. It was now time to focus on the genesis of building a business case that would ultimately become a sales enablement team. And with that, the company found itself at the very beginning of a new and exciting process.

The Business Case: It's All About Alignment

Before you can even begin to build your business case, the first and most important step is gaining support from all of the lines of business across your company. The successful launch of a formalized sales enablement organization will always focus on aligning the departments that will be impacted by and benefit from sales enablement.

Every company has different needs, goals, and objectives when it comes to building a sales enablement business case based upon their company, service offerings, go-to-market needs, and selling motions. The key is to ensure that all of the bases are covered so that your internal customer has a clear and concise understanding of the value of the sales enablement function.

Writing a business case will eventually lead to the creation of your sales enablement charter, where it will be important to clarify which roles and teams will benefit from the sales enablement outputs that your team will own and deliver. For this reason, from the outset you will need to answer these five questions before beginning the charter:

1. Are you focused on decreasing time to revenue or increasing seller productivity?

2. Why is the current process effective or ineffective?

3. Are you utilizing the right resources, processes, programs, platforms, and tools required to create customer-centric sales professionals?

4. What role will your executive sponsor play in supporting the sales enablement function?

5. What is the ideal structure of the sales enablement team in order to serve the needs of your internal customers?

Once you have gathered the answers to these questions, the fun starts! It is time to tackle the six components of the business case. These components are the foundation or blueprint that will ultimately lead to the success of your sales enablement team:

1. Identify, define, and characterize the need for sales enablement

2. Secure executive alignment and support before building the sales enablement team

3. Prepare, review, and align the business case with your executive sponsor prior to presenting it to your internal customers

4. Affirm and clearly articulate company-wide alignment around the roles, responsibilities, and non-responsibilities that will be associated with sales enablement, across all lines of business

5. Ensure that everyone understands and agrees to their responsibilities

6. Establish and document all of the goals, deliverables, Key Performance Indicators (KPIs), and metrics that are critical to future success

Remember that this is just the initial framework; it is partly intended to communicate the value of enablement to your executive sponsor. Creating a successful business case begins with identifying the need for a standalone, comprehensive sales enablement function inside a company. This means that the executive leadership team has already determined the need for consistency and scalability across the company that cannot be achieved by the process that is currently in place.

When creating the business case, always ask how the work and strategy will affect each of the lines of business that it will support. This will allow you to focus on what components to include, which in turn will help you stay focused on the end goal of creating value through scalable and repeatable processes. *Never lose sight of why you are writing the business case.* It should always focus on clarifying problems that the sales enablement team will solve, and how the components will impact revenue.

There are a lot of ways to impact revenue, but the following three desired outcomes have always served me well when presenting sales enablement's value to the senior leadership team:

1. Accelerating speed-to-revenue

2. Increasing individual seller productivity

3. Creating customers for life

Formulating a solid business case involves speaking with—i.e., interviewing—individuals and leaders across many lines of business in the company. The key to a successful interview strategy is to identify a wide cross-section of feedback from your go-to-market teams. This should include non-technical and technical sales, customer success, customer support, customer education, and partner enablement. This will ensure that you get a well-rounded view and variance of feedback.

You will also want to ensure that you interview people with different tenures, levels of experience, professional backgrounds, and history of success. This is important because you will need to ask about specific needs, goals, objectives, and levels of involvement from each of them. *Never assume that you understand what they need.* Always lead with questions that will provide a history of what's been tried, what has worked, and what hasn't worked. There are valuable lessons in each of those answers. This also gives you an opportunity to evaluate current and future resources, processes, programs, and platforms. The end goal of these interviews with your business unit leaders is to ensure that you walk away with an understanding of what they consider to be their essential versus non-essential needs.

While it's important to include all of the company's business unit leaders in your interview process, never forget that your number one internal customer is sales. As the old adage goes, "The further you get from the sun, the colder it gets." NEVER forget that sales is the sun!

The Charter: Focus on Goals and Deliverables

Now that you've assembled the team and outlined its roles and responsibilities, it's time to build the sales enablement charter. One of the most challenging aspects of sales enablement is precisely how to represent its value to the entire organization. It is critical to enlist buy-in from internal customers, secure budget for sales enablement initiatives, and position sales enablement as a valuable business partner. *A sales enablement charter is a strategic overview that defines your team's goals and deliverables.* It is a formalized document that servers three purposes:

1. The charter articulates value to executive leaders and internal customers

2. The charter provides a road map that details all of your internal customers, roles, and responsibilities

3. The charter clearly defines which deliverables are considered out of scope for the sales enablement team

The charter should include your mission statement and start with explaining why the enablement function is critical to the success of the company. It should also include the goals and deliverables of each team member. The charter should answer questions such as: What are the primary problems that sales enablement is trying to solve? What resources are currently in place to solve your internal customer's problems? What additional resources will be needed? As I mentioned before, the charter must also specify deliverables that the sales enablement team is NOT responsible for to ensure clarity around how the sales enablement team will be measured.

The next component is *obstacles*. I recommend brainstorming with other key internal customers to ensure that you're prepared for obstacles that could potentially create barriers to revenue. Keep in mind that obstacles will vary based upon roles, so it is critical to include conversations with each sales segment across your company. This should include Business Development Reps (BDRs), as well as sales professionals by segment, region, and international regions (if your company has a global presence). This will also impact the type of metrics and key performance indicators that will be measured and reported based upon each of the aforementioned sales segments.

One of the most important components of the charter is metrics. The sales enablement charter must serve as an ROI tool for all of your sales enablement activities. With this in mind, the charter should be aligned with your company's goals, deliverables, specific measurements, timelines, and culture. The goal of your team's metrics should be focused on how the sales enablement organization will positively impact your company's revenue.

Metrics can be the most overwhelming component of a sales enablement charter. The key is to focus on things that you can impact. The rest is just noise! There are three key questions to ask when building your metrics section:

- How will your sales enablement activities and programs influence an accelerated path to revenue?

- How will your sales enablement activities and programs increase seller proficiency and productivity?

- How will your sales enablement activities and programs assist in creating customers for life?

We are not talking about smiley sheets, Net Promoter Scores (NPS), and butts in seats anymore. These are simply vanity statistics that fail to show the true value of your sales enablement organization. As with any measurement system, sales enablement metrics can be tricky. You will need to focus on accurate and supportive metrics that help your executive leadership team understand how sales enablement contributes to revenue growth.

There are a lot of ways to show metrics, but they may not align with what success looks like for your leadership team. You should work with your sales leaders to answer the following questions:

- How can sales enablement impact efficiency and effectiveness?

- What are the key milestones and deliverables?

- What happens if you do not achieve the key milestones and deliverables?

I remember working with a sales leader early in my career who was all about sales metrics. He sent me an email requesting a meeting at the beginning of a new quarter so that I could share "the things that my team was working on to influence more closed sales."

This was our first meeting, and I was extremely excited because metrics and analytics were important to me as well. I began by sharing how my team had created new programs and processes to address the way our sales professionals were messaging and positioning our company's solution. This included how many meetings my team had attended, as well as how many times we had measured our sales professionals' success at consistently conveying why a customer should continue doing business with our company. I also shared what my sales enablement team was focused on to improve the success of the sales team in the upcoming quarter.

At this point, the sales leader looked me squarely in the eye and said, "None of this information will help the sales professionals close more business." I was completed devastated. He then said something that I will never forget: "If you want to be successful, ask yourself what's important to a sales leader instead of wasting time, energy, and resources on what you assume will make you and your team look *valuable.*"

At that point, I asked which statistics I should be using instead of the ones I had presented. He smiled and said, "Now you're starting to understand what a partnership really looks like." He then shared the following metrics. From that day forward, these became how my sales enablement team was evaluated:

- Average Deal Size

- Deal Velocity

- New Pipeline Created

- Number of Closed Deals

- Time to First Close for New Hires

- Win Rates

I learned from this meeting that not every statistic is valuable; some are just numbers. I also learned that sales enablement is about asking the questions that lead to valuable answers for your internal customers. It is critical to provide your internal customers with supportive, valuable, and agreed-upon metrics. The last thing you want to do is give them what YOU think they need.

Collaboration with your key internal customers can be achieved by creating a joint execution strategy. You can agree, in writing, on how the sales enablement organization will measure success. There are three questions that must be answered in order to gain agreement before moving into the implementation phase:

- How does sales enablement define success?

- What short-, medium-, and long-term milestones are critical to meet the definition of success?

- What is sales enablement's impact on accelerating speed-to-revenue, increasing sales efficiency, and creating customers for life?

Now that you have outlined the components, collaborated with your internal customers to define success criteria, and agreed upon the metrics and measurements, it is time to create an implementation plan. The sole purpose of this implementation plan is to ensure that both the sales enablement organization and its internal customers are held accountable, while building in flexibility for growth as the company and team matures.

Finally, iterate, iterate, iterate! As with any process or tool, your sales enablement charter is a living, breathing document that has to be updated and communicated regularly. As your business grows and matures, you will need to ensure that your sales enablement charter grows and matures as well. I recommend scheduling a review with your internal customers at least twice per year to ensure alignment. This will not only ensure that your sales enablement charter is relevant, but that it aligns with the maturation cycle of your company. This review cycle will also prevent your sales enablement organization from falling into the "this is the way it's always been done" trap.

Now that you have created your charter, all of the internal players should understand the value of sales enablement, as well as their specific roles, responsibilities, and deliverables. It is now time to shift focus to the most important success driver: aligning all of your sales enablement activities to your buyer's journey.

Chapter 6

ALIGNING SALES ENABLEMENT TO YOUR BUYER'S JOURNEY

WE NOT ONLY NEED TO UNDERSTAND THE DEMOGRAPHIC OF OUR CUSTOMERS, BUT WE NEED TO MAKE SURE THAT WE CREATE DIFFERENT CONTENT FOR EACH OF THE DIFFERENT STAGES OF THE BUYER'S JOURNEY.

—*Kyle Gray*

A common problem I see time and again is that companies are unable to establish alignment between the buyer's journey and their selling motions. This includes their sales process, sales methodology, sales stages, and sales enablement tools. This is where a sales enablement practitioner really has the opportunity to shine! Sales enablement can diagnose problems, pull all of the components together, and coordinate all of the lines of business required to create a solution.

Let's dig a little deeper into the components of the buyer's journey. It all begins with answering two basic questions.

- What is the buyer's journey?

- Why is it important for salespeople and marketers to understand the buyer's journey?

It All Begins and Ends With the Buyer's Journey

Figure 6: The Buyer's Journey Framework

The buyer's journey includes the common steps that a buyer progresses through when making a decision. In order to build sales enablement tools and strategies around this journey, we must begin with aligning the journey to your company's sales stages, methodology, and process. Remember, it all begins and ends with the customer. As long as that is your focus, you will never go wrong!

Understanding each stage of the journey can also help sales and marketing professionals collaborate and deliver joint customer-centric strategies. When you're familiar with the ins and outs of the buyer's journey, you're in a position to make the buying experience productive for them, plus more readily avoid potential dangers that can impede their decision to make a purchase.

I once worked with a mid-size tech company that was struggling to increase their Average Contract Value (ACV) of sales. Together we were able to identify the problem: Due to fear of losing sales, their sales professionals were quickly offering prospects a deep level of discount. After meeting with the sales professionals, I realized that this resulted from an inability to handle the prospect's objections.

I worked with the sales leaders to outline the specific objections that were creating panic. I then worked with the marketing and competitive analysis teams to create assets and a workshop that prepared the sales professionals to address the objections rather than resorting to unnecessary discounts. If I learned anything from this situation, it's that discounts are only required in the absence of value being understood by the prospect.

This is just one example of how I have seen the buyer's journey successfully tied to a company's selling process. Let's take a look at the stages of the journey.

The Buyer's Journey: Identify, Assess, Prioritize, Solidify, Maintain

I like to divide the buyer's journey into these five stages, but keep in mind that the stage names and decision criteria will vary depending upon your company's maturation cycle, selling motions, and of course product or service offerings. Let's dig a bit into the typical progression of these stages.

Buyer's Journey Stage 1: Identify the Problem

This stage is all about helping the prospect identify the concerns or problems that are either detracting from productivity and efficiency or creating pain. The initial questions to ask the buyer are: What are your key concerns? What problems must be solved? What tools, products, and/or services are required to solve these key concerns? What will happen if these key concerns are not solved?

These are generally the most pressing questions, and I guarantee that these are keeping your buyers awake at night. The sales professional's job is NOT to answer these questions right away, but instead to ask questions that will give insights into how painful the problem is and what it will take to administer the correct medicine to alleviate their pain.

Buyer's Journey Stage 2: Assess Possible Solutions

Now that the prospect has confirmed that there is a need for change, the next stage is all about helping them assess the best ways to alleviate the current state of pain, while also assessing the cost of inaction; i.e., what will happen if they don't make changes.

Once the prospect has made these baseline assessments, your sales professionals should have enough data to solidify this second stage of the sales process, which includes identifying goals, objectives, needs, key decision makers, competitors, and budget. This stage should provide your salespeople with enough answers, insights, and data to assess the selling motions, activity milestones, and sales enablement tools required to label a prospect as a validated opportunity. Now it is time to move into the prioritization stage.

Buyer's Journey Stage 3: Prioritize the Solution

Now that the prospect has confirmed the need for change (identify) and answered the assessment questions (assess), it's time to focus on prioritizing the activities that will move them toward finding a solution to their problem(s). This is the stage where I have seen problematic, stagnated, and even killed deals. This is because most sales professionals are able to uncover needs during the discovery and qualification phase, but few are equipped to address and prioritize solutions once the problem is diagnosed.

The key to prioritizing solutions is the ability to truly hear and listen to prospects. This is where your sales enablement organization has an opportunity to show its highest level of value to your sales leadership team. Sales enablement can teach the skills of staying curious and asking open-ended questions. This stage of the process takes Q&A and puts it on steroids. It's not just enough to ask questions and be curious; salespeople must continuously uncover the prospects' needs by guiding them to provide information that is important to them. Once this is achieved, it is the sales professional's job to share your company's form of customized pain relief. And with that, it is time to pivot to the solution solidification phase!

Buyer's Journey Stage 4: Solidify the Solution

Stage four is often the most difficult part of aligning the sales cycle to the buyer's journey. The sales professional has now done the heavy lifting of identifying the problem and tying the prospect's pain or needs to your company's key differentiation, competitive advantage, and business value. Now it's time to solidify the prospect's attachment to your company's solution. This is where sales professionals must exhibit the highest level of compassion, empathy, and emotional intelligence by showing that your company's solution provides both a personal and company-level win for their buyer.

I have seen that most sales professionals don't do a very good job of tying the purchase to a personal level of win for their buyer. Sure, they talk about how it can accelerate speed-to-revenue, increase productivity and efficiency, and on occasion dig deep into the cost of inaction. But often this isn't enough of a reason for a person to move forward with purchasing a new solution. What often drives a buyer to make a purchase is when the prospect articulates, in depth, why making this purchase will be advantageous for *them*. This could mean a promotion, a bigger voice, or in some cases a seat at the decision table. Never underestimate the value of uncovering and highlighting the personal win for the buyer.

Once the sales professional has successfully solidified the solution, it's time to finalize this fourth stage of the process, which on the sales side should include a strategy overview, solution terms, finalized pricing negotiations, and a signed contract. Now it is time to move it into the often-overlooked maintenance stage.

Buyer's Journey Stage 5: Maintain Satisfaction

While we call this the maintenance stage, it's more like the build-a-customer-for-life stage. Now that the prospect has decided upon your company's solution, the final part of their buyer's journey is deciding whether to stick with this solution for the long term.

This should be the *easy* part. Unfortunately, most sales professionals do a poor job of transitioning the prospect into their company's customer success organization. Most sales professionals are focused on closing their next deal, so the transition meeting with their counterparts or customer success manager is either done ineffectively or not at all.

The best implementations that I have experienced actually began *before* the sale closed. The customer success manager was introduced to the customer during the latter part of the solidification phase, once the contract was signed. This created a natural transitional introduction between the customer and the customer success manager. The early introduction also allowed for the customer success manager to be viewed by the customer as a part of the sales team rather than an unknown entity.

This is where sales enablement can really earn our place at the table with sales: by being the orchestra master between sales and customer success. Why invest so much time, energy, and resources into closing a deal only to let it all fall apart because of a poor or nonexistent transition process? The sales enablement organization should work as an intermediary between the sales and customer success or account management organization to create a scalable and repeatable transition process that focuses on ONE thing, ensuring that the customer feels like they made the right decision by agreeing to purchase a solution from your company. According to Salesforce.com, 72% of customers will share their good experiences with others. As it has been said, "No amount of money can buy a happy customer."

Tactics and Strategies to Support the Buyer's Journey

Now that we have a better understanding of the buyer's journey, we can see that the sales enablement organization can shine by aligning all of your internal teams to focus on helping the customer. For companies engaged in complex sales with extended sales cycles, be sure to examine the Business-to-Business (B2B) customer journey. Map out the areas where prospects drop out of the funnel. Never forget that it's critical to focus on how you can decrease their pain or increase their efficiency. Concentrate on how you can make your customer and their business more successful, then create a streamlined process between all the business units in your company—human resources, sales, marketing—to create a smooth buyer's journey.

We all want a seamless customer experience. Yet our companies are full of interdepartmental seams. If you want to know how to improve the customer experience, sales enablement must learn to communicate, collaborate, and orchestrate across the multiple lines of business. Let's examine some of the most important sales enablement components that form the baseline of how things should be done in the 3.0 era. These strategies and tactics include:

1. Reset your Ideal Customer Profile (ICP)

2. Create an airtight end-to-end process

3. Stay top of mind with prospects and customers without being annoying

4. Implement an in-depth discovery and qualification process

5. Help prospects with the decision to move forward

6. Build accreditations or certifications designed to validate learning experiences

Let's examine each of these in turn. Together these tactics and strategies, if implemented correctly, will help propel your organization into the 3.0 era.

Reset Your Ideal Customer Profile (ICP): This is usually the first step in any sales process, for good reason. It's impossible to sell if you don't know who will buy your products or services! While the ICP is a critical and widely recognized component of sales, unfortunately it is one of the components that dies a slow death because it's rarely updated. This is a HUGE mistake!

In alignment with the best practices of some of the world's most successful companies, the ICP should be an iterative process, not a static process as I have seen all too often. Based upon the speed of business, product releases, competitive landscape, go-to-market updates, and mergers and acquisitions, your company's ICP should be updated at least twice per year.

Selling today requires a stronger partnership between sales, marketing, and sales enablement. Think about this process as your favorite vehicle. Marketing is the beautiful exterior that makes you so proud to drive around in it. However, the vehicle also requires gas, tune-ups, and regularly scheduled maintenance to keep in top condition. This is where sales enablement comes in. It is your job as a sales enablement practitioner to ensure that the vehicle receives maintenance so that it can perform at its highest levels. Regularly updating the ICP is an important component of that maintenance.

Create an airtight end-to-end process: As I mentioned previously, buyers are far more informed and savvier than ever before. According to Jeff Davis, consultant, global keynote speaker, and author of the book *Create Togetherness*, "In order to drive successful growth, companies must have a strategic roadmap for B2B leaders ready to take on the challenge of aligning their sales and marketing teams to win the business of modern buyers."

This has never been truer than it is today. It is critical that your company's messaging and positioning, go-to-market strategy, and short, medium, and long-term sales enablement metrics are aligned. Back to the car analogy, if one part of the car is broken, then the entire car suffers. Sales professionals are counting on all of the lines of business to collaborate and build an easy-to-follow strategy that will ultimately lead to success for them, their prospects, and their customers.

Implement an in-depth Discovery and Qualification process: When engaging potential customers, we normally focus on three things: *key differentiation, competitive advantage, and business value.* Companies are usually great at the first two, but customers really only care about the last one, business value. And the best way to figure out how to provide value is by really connecting with the prospect and listening to their needs. Yet all too many sales professionals still approach the discovery and qualification process as a *feature dump* of features, benefits, and bells and whistles designed to impress the prospect. When done correctly, discovery and qualification should be an opportunity to build rapport, identify problems, and tie your company's service offerings to solving the prospect's problems.

The buyer's access to information, data points, and research tools has added a significant amount of complexity to the buying cycle, which in turn has slowed down the overall sales process. According to the Miller Heiman Group, "More than 70 percent of B2B buyers fully define their needs before engaging with a sales representative, and almost half identify specific solutions before reaching out."

It is therefore critically important that sales professionals understand the prospect's key decision points within the buying cycle. This might include: Who is involved in the decision process? What is the compelling reason for buying? What is their established budget? Who are the key decision makers and how will buying your product or service help to either increase productivity or decrease pain? It is equally as important to understand the personal impact of the potential purchase. Always ensure that your sales professionals are asking questions that will help them assess both the personal and company impact on their buyers.

Stay top-of-mind with prospects and customers without being annoying: Leading with empathy, compassion, and emotional intelligence has never meant more in the business landscape than it does today. The same can be said for selling. No one has a 100% close rate, and the sales cycle is slower than it once was. With that in mind, it's critical for sales professionals to keep prospects warm until the timing is right. Here are some sales best practices to stay relevant with prospects and customers:

1. Focus on helping, not selling: Remember, it is the job of the sales professional to listen, learn, then lead—not close business simply to meet their sales quota. Every sales motion should be focused on meeting the prospect or customer's needs.

2. Continue curating and sharing content: Keep it simple by summarizing your content into three or four bullets. The content should include three elements: What do I want them to think? What do I want them to feel? What do I want them to do? Every prospect or customer interaction should end with a call to action.

3. Nurture now for future success: Selling is a process that rarely culminates in a single conversation. Just as in real-life situations (okay, let's call it what it is, dating), it's unrealistic to go into a first meeting with the expectation of a marriage proposal. But budgets and mindsets are rarely frozen permanently. Ensure that your content is useful and memorable so that you're relevant whenever your prospects and customers are ready to engage again.

4. Every interaction must have value: According to John Barrows, CEO of JBarrows Sales Training, "The act of checking in or doing pulse checks with a prospect or customer has absolutely no value during the sales cycle and could lead to a short relationship with them." Be sure that you're tying all social media and outbound communications to business outcomes.

5. Share content from thought leaders outside their industry: This will show that you're an informed and well-versed resource.

Focus on the personal impacts of buying (or not buying): As I mentioned earlier, relationships are the backbone of success. The best sales professionals focus on the value of their products and solutions to not only the company, but the individual buyer. If there's anything that I have learned as a sales enablement practitioner, it's that people buy from, and because of, personal relationships with people. The ability to focus on helping rather than selling or closing a sale directly correlates to stronger relationships, which ultimately leads to increased closed sales.

It is therefore important to help prospects make a decision, even if the decision is to not buy. This shows empathy and compassion, and it also helps to strengthen the level of rapport with the prospect. Even if they're not moving forward with a sale, they might come back to you in the future when their needs and situation are different.

Build accreditations or certifications designed to validate learning experiences: Sales professionals often struggle to tie the company's products and solutions to a prospect or customer's needs or pain points. Most of the time it's not because the sales professional doesn't understand how the product or solution works. It usually comes down to a lack of enablement around how to diagnose and address the prospect's pain level.

This is where a sales enablement practitioner has an opportunity to partner with sales, marketing, and product marketing to create an accreditation or certification. The goal is to create a consistent validation point that confirms the sales professional's ability to articulate value, diagnose a prospect's pain points, and ultimately provide a solution. The solution sometimes equates to Tylenol. Other times, it equates to Vicodin, and in extreme cases, it equates to an extraction or amputation. A successful sales professional is able to diagnose the type of problem and instantly apply the correct level of relief.

Assessing a sales professional's ability to diagnose problems and administer solutions requires accreditations or certifications that are tied to specific scoring criteria designed to drive consistency in the delivery of your company's messaging and positioning. Certifications are awarded by educational programs or academic institutions, and they're generally reserved for technical roles within a company, such as sales consultants and engineers. Accreditations are formal, independent verifications used within the company, and they are typically facilitated by a sales enablement team and used to validate a seller's ability to provide the appropriate messaging and positioning to a prospect or customer.

The strategic implementation of accreditations is important because they differentiate enablement outcomes from vanity statistics. Accreditations help ensure that each sales enablement activity is strategically tied to revenue-generating metrics and key performance indicators to substantiate the value of the sale enablement team.

★

All of the above strategies and tactics form the foundation of how sales enablement provides value in the 3.0 era. Sales enablement practitioners must be viewed as an extension of the sales teams, while simultaneously being a valued partner across all of the business units within a company.

Each sales enablement activity must be strategically tied to revenue-generating metrics and KPIs to substantiate the value of the sale enablement team. In the 3.0 era, sales enablement practitioners are so much more than schedulers, trainers, and the fixers of broken things. Sales enablement offers unique and invaluable strategies that link sales enablement to a deep understanding of—and appreciation for—the buyer's journey.

Chapter 7:

SALES ENABLEMENT AS COMMUNICATIONS CENTER

*THE BIGGEST PROBLEM IN COMMUNICATION
IS THE ILLUSION THAT IT HAS TAKEN PLACE.*
—*George Bernard Shaw*

It is impossible to truly understand the impact of sales enablement without understanding the three key components that I call the Holy Trinity: communication, collaboration, and orchestration. They are the foundation upon which all successful sales enablement organizations, processes, programs, tools, and platforms are built.

As with any successful journey, the sales enablement process always begins with a strategic communications plan. The level of success of your sales enablement program is based upon understanding your Ideal Customer Profile (ICP), as discussed in the previous chapter. Once this all-important baseline is established, the entire sales enablement process will revolve around the art and science of communicating, collaborating, and orchestrating across your multiple lines of business.

The Sales Enablement Trinity: Communication, Collaboration, Orchestration

Communication: Communication is defined as the process of passing information and understanding from one person to another. In other words, it is the process of transmitting and sharing ideas, opinions, facts, values, etc., from one person to another, or from one organization to another.

Within the sales enablement context, there is an important distinction between sharing your thoughts and ideas with your internal business unit leaders versus designing and deploying an actual communications plan. The latter includes communicating your goals across all of the lines of business in a clear, concise manner that aligns directly with your company's corporate goals and initiatives. This ability to communicate clearly across multiple departments is what sets sales enablement apart, and it is therefore a skill that must be emphasized and nurtured.

All too often, the problem with business relationships is that people don't listen with the intent to understand; they listen with the intent to reply. This is the biggest mistake that a sales enablement practitioner can make, because it leads us (okay, let's be honest, it is usually our ego) to believe that we know what our customers need better than they do. I have seen credibility and partnerships ruined—not to mention many well-intended programs go down in flames—because the sales enablement team gave sales professionals what they *assumed* was the answer rather than taking time to explore the problems and working collaboratively to solve them.

Rule number one as a sales enablement practitioner is to *always* remember that you have one mouth and two ears for a reason. Your value will increase when you learn to listen more and talk less!

When working with your internal customers, the key to ongoing success is to ask questions confirming that you heard what they said and understand what they meant. There is nothing worse than walking out of a meeting *assuming* that you're all on the same page, only to find out later that you made an incorrect assumption. To avoid this fate, my recommendation is to follow a simple three-step formula:

1. Ask your internal customers a question.

2. Repeat their answer back to them in their words.

3. Confirm that what you repeated is exactly what they said to you.

You will be amazed at how many wasted resource hours this simple process will save you. If you ask questions the right way, you will walk away with a laundry list of deliverables, and then the real work, not to mention angst and anxiety, begins.

How do you translate communications skills into strategic, long-term, scalable, and repeatable processes? I always begin with a simple philosophy: "It takes many ideas to create one great strategy." My most memorable career successes always came from sharing my ideas and allowing others, regardless of level or title, to add their thoughts and life experiences to the strategy.

When you have a thought, idea, or strategy, remember that it is only that—YOURS. That doesn't mean it's the most effective or efficient way to get things done; it's merely the way that YOU know how to do it. If you want to gain support, start by listening, not talking. I have learned that most people genuinely want to be helpful once they are shown that their input has value.

The larger number of people in a conversation, the more each of the participants will work to have their needs expressed, opinions heard, and sometimes political agendas interjected into decisions. The role of the sales enablement professional is to ensure that there is a balance between allowing others to be heard and not allowing any individual or line of business to dominate the overall process. This is where you as a sales enablement practitioner have an opportunity to add enormous value.

I remember working with a financial services company that was looking to expand globally. After a couple of meetings, I realized that their company's biggest competition was not external; it was actually between their internal lines of business. My initial goal had been to bring sales, marketing, product marketing, product management, and human resources together for a working session focused on an upcoming product release. Little did they realize at the time that their own communication habits were the key to a successful release.

The meeting began with the product marketing leader outlining how the messaging and positioning was changing. I noticed that the other leaders showed a complete disinterest in this approach. Many began checking emails on their phone. This was followed by the sales leader announcing how frustrated he was at not being asked for *real world* customer examples and pain points that could be used to drive the direction and components of this product release. At this point I could feel the animosity and frustration in the room. Then it was time for the product management leader to outline the components of the release cycle. Again, some of the other meeting participants were checking their emails.

It was time to disrupt what clearly was their normal process. I asked each of the participants to answer two questions: How did they feel this process was going? How could it be improved? As you can imagine, there were a number of answers that all emphasized frustration over a particular group having more control over the overall process. I walked up to the whiteboard in the front of the room and wrote a single statement over and over. That statement was, *CUSTOMER FIRST!* It was at that moment that the proverbial lightbulb turned on for each of the participants. Their mindset and the course of the meeting instantly shifted. It was a simple reminder that no business unit was more important than the other in this process, and that winning is truly a team sport.

Your role as a sales enablement practitioner is to balance out feedback, input, ideas, and sometimes political agendas. But you are not a referee. You need to remain objective while also ensuring that everyone feels that their voices are heard and acknowledged during the process. Clear communication is based upon how it is received as well as how it is shared. With this in mind, develop the skill of speaking in such a way that others love to listen to you, and listen in a way that others love to speak with you.

Collaboration: The sales enablement organization must be the hub that spokes out to every part of the organization. This means partnering closely with the sales, marketing, product marketing, product management, sales operations, and human resources organizations to ensure that they're collaborating like a well-oiled machine. This also means working with your key internal customers to define and agree upon the roles and responsibilities that lead to success. Once those are agreed upon, it is important to outline the metrics that will be utilized to validate sales enablement's value.

While your goals, deliverables, and metrics are often determined by the sales leader, you must never forget that the other lines of business are counting on you to be a partner as well. You must see the holes in your systems and work to streamline communication in order to alleviate the flaws. One person or small team can make a huge difference in the customer's experience as well as enable a company to adapt and customize its strengths effectively. That is one of the responsibilities of the sales enablement organization. Oftentimes, we as sales enablement practitioners are not the owners of revenue metrics, but we are expected to assist the sales professionals to meet and exceed these goals.

This is where the ability to influence and sometimes persuade is the best tool in your sales enablement toolbox. I have found that the best way to drive cross-functional collaboration is through the creation of a *sales enablement council.* The goal of this council is to bring together all of the key contributors that play a role in creating a successful sales environment.

The participants in the council should include marketing, product marketing, product management, sales, human resources, and sales enablement, and the council meeting should be facilitated on a monthly basis. The agenda should be focused on discussing hiring cycles, upcoming events, product releases, competitive updates, and any changes since the last meeting. The monthly meeting ensures that all of the lines of business are in sync around goals, deliverables, and metrics as it relates to the events scheduled around the annual enablement calendar. The meeting also gives each of the lines of business an opportunity to share wins, updates, and changes.

It's amazing how these collaborative meetings build relationships and trust. Alliances can be forged between organizations that in some companies are seen as adversaries.

As mentioned before, the ability to influence and persuade is one of the best tools in your sales enablement toolbox. In order to know when, where, and most importantly *why* you need to utilize this tool at the right time, you will need to answer the following questions:

- How will you maintain balance across the lines of business without alienating or creating friction?

- How will you work to ensure that there is cohesion across the lines of business?

- Who should be integrated into the process of building your sales enablement programs and processes?

- How often should you be coordinating with each of your lines of business?

- How do you show the value of your sales enablement organization to each of these partners in their language, not in sales enablement speak?

- How do you integrate these partners, not only in the design and deployment stage, but in the reinforcement and iteration stages of your programs?

Never confuse activity with productivity. Just because you and your sales enablement organization are constantly busy, or even overwhelmed for that matter, doesn't mean that the company sees, acknowledges, or validates all of your activity. The company may see a lot going on within your organization but never actually equate it to productivity or meeting their needs. But when you establish clear avenues of communication and collaboration between the lines of business, you create a natural means of showing and sharing productivity, value, and success.

Orchestration: Indian politician and cricketer Navjot Singh Sidhu once said, "You can't play a symphony alone. It takes an orchestra to play it." There could not be a better characterization of the role of sales enablement across a company. Sales enablement is the conductor that ensures the various instruments are played in sync to create beautiful, productive, scalable, and repeatable pieces of music.

Orchestration is defined as "the planning or coordination of the elements of a situation to produce a desired effect or outcome." Let's think about the lines of business within your company. You have brass (sales), woodwinds (marketing), percussion (human resources), and strings (product marketing). They're all playing notes, albeit some are out of tune while others are playing on top of each other. This will continue until sales enablement steps up to the podium, taps the stand, and organizes all of the noise into a beautiful piece of music.

The sales enablement organization is the conductor of your company's orchestra. Our job is to collaborate with each of the lines of business to ensure that their notes are played at the right time, pace, and volume to create a pleasing melody for our prospects and customers. We must collaborate and interact with each department differently. We collaborate with marketing and product marketing to provide direct feedback from prospects and customers around how the company's messaging and positioning statements are resonating in the *real world*. We interact with product management to provide relevant feedback around specific product feature requests from prospects and customers. We interact with sales and human resources to provide updates regarding the success or lack of success with hiring practices.

Given our level of direct interaction with both newly hired and legacy sales professionals, it's critical that we constantly update both of these groups regarding success or a need for adjustment. We interact with product management, customer success, professional services, and customer support to receive feedback from customers that can be incorporated into future enablement processes, programs, and platforms. We interact with partners and alliances to ensure that we are enabling our sales professionals and external sale partners around the value and process of joint selling to meet the needs of our prospects and customers.

In essence, we're collaborating with every group that has a touchpoint across the customer journey to ensure that the company is on the same page and focused on creating a beautiful piece of music.

Sales Enablement: The Ambassador Between Departments

While each department within a company plays a significant role in creating and fostering a successful sales team, let's take a moment to focus on the interaction between sales and marketing. Marketing is responsible for driving the assets that will provide sales with qualified leads, while sales is focused on validating and driving those leads to increase closed deals. In order for leads to move toward closed sales and additional revenue, these lines of business must be reading from the same sheet of music. Not only must they be on the same page, but they must be in sync with the conductor in order to know when to add their specialty to the musical selection.

When sales and marketing work in the same direction, with a well-defined handoff and tracking process, this removes friction, removes selling obstacles, reduces frustration, and accelerate speed-to-revenue. When sales and marketing communicate clearly and work cohesively toward the same goals, that is what we call *alignment*. While this may sound like nirvana, it is achievable with the right sales enablement leader at the front of the orchestra.

Now of course that is the best-case scenario. Unfortunately, more often than not, it rarely happens so smoothly. What does it look like when the instruments (lines of business) are out of sync? The most common scenario is when your marketing team brings in leads but your sales team can't close them. The reasons may vary from incomplete qualification to inconsistency with your company's Ideal Customer Profile. Sometimes the individual teams at your organization are not aligned around the same Key Performance Indicators (KPIs). Other times the lines of business are all trying to do the right thing for the customer, at the same time, without anyone working to check that they're not stepping over each other. Whatever the source, this is how disconnects and silos are created.

I have realized over my career that KPIs are generally not the root of the problem. It usually comes down to a lack of clear communication around roles, responsibilities, goals, deliverables, and metrics. Imagine that the sales teams are constantly complaining about receiving bad leads from the marketing team, but they never take the time to define what a good lead looks like. Meanwhile, the marketing team ignores the complaints from sales. They continue to share what they believe to be good leads, all while complaining about the sales team's inability to close sales around the leads that were provided.

This all creates a vicious circle of unproductive complaining. If not addressed, it will erode the relationship between sales and marketing. I have seen this scenario play out far too many times, and the interesting thing is that there's a very simple fix. It requires a nonpartisan organization—you guessed it, sales enablement—to bring everyone together with the goal of creating and agreeing upon a clear definition of what will be considered a *qualified* lead. See? It's simple, as long as sales enablement is on the scene!

Another area where cooperation between lines of business is important is **territory management.** The focus should be on things like how you're building your pipeline, defining the right target, pipeline growth guidelines that include a handoff process between roles, pipeline tracking, and finally, how sales collaborates with account management to ensure that customers are implementing what they have purchased. Each line of business must constantly and concisely communicate with the other to ensure customer satisfaction. A closed sale is never the end of the customer's journey.

★

I have always been enamored with languages and cultures, and one of my favorite parts of running a global sales enablement team has been the opportunity to travel globally. Travel is enriching for the soul. It provides a window into other climates and cultures. Over the years, I have come to see sales enablement itself as a form of travel, where we become the translators of dialects and languages. We speak to sales, marketing, product marketing, product management, customer success and support, and human resources in their own language, not in sales enablement jargon.

As translators and travelers, it is important to gain enough credibility with sales professionals to be invited to participate in prospect and customer meetings—without fear that you might do or say something that derails the sale! One of my fondest memories was during a debrief meeting with a sales leader and sales professional after one of the largest deals of that quarter was closed. The sales leader asked the sales professional what role I had played in helping to close the deal. The sales professional replied, "There's something to be said for a sales enablement guy speaking our language and making the prospect feel comfortable enough to say yes."

As sales enablement professionals, we aren't closing deals, but we still have an opportunity to impact deals while gaining credibility with sales professionals. As you can imagine, the next couple of weeks were filled with meeting requests from other sales professionals, now that I had earned my stripes in the aforementioned meeting.

Working as the orchestrator between departments often involves getting out of your office and spending time in the field in order to get an intimate understanding of what your prospects and customers are experiencing. When you actually stick your feet in the dirt, you learn to not only hear but listen for the key pain points that are being shared with your sales professionals. That is where the translation begins. You then take the feedback to marketing and let them know how the content, corporate pitch, and competitive information is being received by prospects and customers. If you see any opportunities to enhance the content, you will need to be very specific.

For example, let's say the company pitch is really resonating well externally, but when we get to slide seven, we are creating confusion and uncertainty. Can we either tighten up the wording or remove it completely in order to keep the prospect or customer engaged in the conversation? Or let's say you have met with a fair number of prospects and customers, and you're noticing that the same feature and upgrade is being discussed or asked for repetitively. It's your job as a translator to take that information back to the product management group and ask where that particular feature or upgrade sits on the product release cycle.   The last thing you want is to discover a problem that's not being addressed, only to find that your competitors are now winning deals over your company simply because they heard, listened, and took immediate action while your company was still strategizing around how and when to release this feature. It's critical to bring information to each of your departments in the language that they speak so that they understand the urgency and the value of decisive action.

Communication, collaboration, and orchestration truly lay the groundwork for implementing world-class sales enablement programs. While these may seem like small things or "soft skills," what they actually do is establish a foundation of rapport and trust that becomes important for each and every sales enablement activity.

Chapter 8

THE ART AND SCIENCE OF ONBOARDING

COMING TOGETHER IS THE BEGINNING, STAYING TOGETHER IS THE PROCESS, AND WORKING TOGETHER IS THE SUCCESS!
—*Henry Ford*

Every successful sports coach will tell you that games aren't won on the field, court, or ice, but rather during the strategic planning phase. The game itself culminates in the flawless execution of all of the practice that occurred prior to the game. The same can be said for sales enablement. Running a world-class sales enablement program requires an enormous amount of planning to ensure that you have the right people, resources, and tools in place to successfully execute on your scope, vision, goals, and deliverables. And as I discussed in chapter 4, the most important part of the planning process is the first of the 5 Ps—and that, of course, is people.

When it comes to *talent assessment and acquisition,* it's all about ensuring that your company has the right people in place for today and the future. If the shift to selling in a virtual environment has not impacted your company already, it will soon touch every part of the business landscape, beginning with the talent assessment and selection process. Once your company has defined or updated its Ideal Employee Profile (IEP), it's time to begin designing, deploying, measuring, and iterating its sales onboarding program.

Sales Onboarding: The Pathway to Continued Success

Onboarding is the foundation of every career and the initial entryway into a company. As such, your sales onboarding program must be aligned with your company's new hire orientation. As it has been said, "You get one chance to make a first impression." This could not be more accurate than when it comes to your company's onboarding program. It should feel like a funnel, starting with a general company overview and progressively getting closer to the ground by transitioning into sales-specific content.

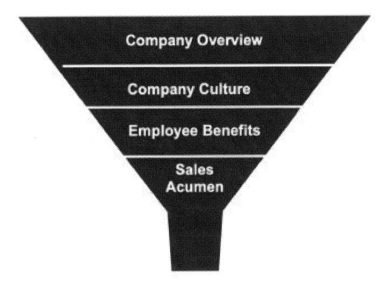

Figure 7: Sales Onboarding Alignment

The alignment of your onboarding and orientation programs should reinforce for the newly hired sales professional that they have joined the right company. From day one, they must feel that they're being set up for a long, successful sales career. The company onboarding and sales-specific programs should feel like continuous chapters in the same book. One of the biggest mistakes I have seen in onboarding is that the new hire orientation and sales onboarding programs feel choppy and disjointed.

I was once hired by a company that was in the midst of a hyper-growth period. One of the key selling points of their recruiting team was that the executive leadership team had remained engaged throughout the company's growth phase. I was excited by this because I had previously worked with companies at the same maturation point, and this level of executive engagement was the first thing to disappear. I walked into the company orientation with the expectation of intimate exchange with some, if not all, of the executive leadership team. Unfortunately, this never happened.

Instead, I (along with the other newly hired employees) was subjected to a revolving carousel of endless PowerPoint slides that included high-level and, in some cases, outdated information about their business units. There was very little audience engagement, and I left the orientation meeting feeling like I had joined a completely different company than the one that recruited me.

The one saving grace was the highly interactive and engaging sales boot camp that followed. While this was an impressive event, it left me wondering how the two programs were so different. The contrast culminated in a confusing and frustrating onboarding experience. This was the incentive I needed to immediately engage with our human resources team to begin working on ensuring that no new hire would have an onboarding experience similar to mine.

★

Onboarding is all about creating a baseline of learning that will lead to continued success. While the individual components of your sales onboarding program will continually shift based upon your company's maturation cycle, go-to-market strategy, mergers, acquisitions, competitive landscape shifts, and product releases, I recommend that you always design and build your sales onboarding program based upon the lifecycle of a sale.

Important components of an onboarding program include:

- An overview of business value

- An overview of KPIs

- Building an internal network

- Tools, messaging, and positioning

- Role-specific breakouts that expose sales professionals to each component of the sales process

If you work in a globally distributed company, you will include a virtual approach to sales onboarding, which should include the same components. As the world continues to shift to a more remote selling environment, sales enablement professionals must find ways to foster a sense of community, belonging, and support throughout the onboarding experience. This is the part of the process that you will want to spend most of your time designing. During the design phase, ensure that all of your components will educate, entertain, and keep the sales professionals engaged. As the old adage goes, "Measure twice and cut once."

When designing an internal sales onboarding program, it's so important to ask your sales leaders what they need, what causes them the most pain, and what their selling obstacles are.

I REPEAT:

INCLUDE YOUR SALES LEADERS IN THE PROCESS. This is so important that it requires bold AND shouty caps! You should NOT design your sales onboarding program in a vacuum unless you want to give sales *what YOU think they need*, thereby sabotaging all of your credibility with them. I would recommend that you share your proposed program with your sales leaders early and often. You will be amazed at how supportive they will be if you simply take time to ask for their input. Once you have received this input, create a framework around your proposed program and solicit their feedback again.

While we're on the topic of initial rollouts, I highly recommend building a pilot or beta program into your design strategy. This will allow you to deploy the sales onboarding program in a small region or to a limited number of users. A pilot program gives you an opportunity to adjust, iterate, enhance, and in some cases remove entire sections of the program. Just don't expect your pilot to be your best work. Honestly, it will likely be something you look back at later in your career and have a good laugh at!

I have shared a number of sales enablement stories that later became best practices. Well, this is not one of those stories. The first time I facilitated a sales boot camp as a trainer, I had recently joined Siebel Systems and was ready to make my mark on the world! I had done all of my due diligence by sharing my program with each of the sales leaders to guarantee that I had their support and buy-in. As the day approached, I became more and more excited to connect with my first-ever cohort.

I spent the night before the workshop carefully arranging all of the company-based tchotchkes, pens, tablets, etc., across each table. When the students arrived that morning, they were greeted with a beautiful breakfast spread. When the workshop began, I opened with the traditional introductions, workshop overview, and ice-breaker exercises. I was just about to introduce my first presenter when... THE PROJECTOR DIED!

Now I'm standing in front of a room full of newly hired sales professionals expecting to be trained without a working projector. This was the one thing I had not planned for. I had two options: freeze up and lose credibility for the remainder of the workshop, or get creative and keep them entertained. I quickly moved toward the second option. I place them into small groups and instructed them to answer the following four questions.

- Who traveled the furthest to attend the workshop?

- What special talent do you have that no one in the room would ever guess?

- What are you hoping to get out of this workshop?

- What was your first impression when the projector died?

I then asked each participant to select a partner. Everyone would have to share their partner's answers with the group. This all provided me just enough time to slip out of the room and find someone from the audio-visual group to assist with the projector—which they did in a remarkably speedy manner!

While I can laugh now, as I have many times, about this experience, it actually taught me a very serious lesson. This could have all gone in a completely different direction if my first training was a disaster for the company. Instead, that day I learned to expect the best but prepare for the worst, and that even bad scenarios are learning opportunities. After that incident, you can bet that I make sure there's always an audio-visual resource in the room.

I don't remember the name of the person from the audio-visual department, but if you're reading this book, thank you for saving my career!

This story always reminds me that it's important to continuously mitigate risk so that you expose your shortcomings and mistakes to the smallest number of learners. Here are five critical questions that will help you mitigate risk and build a clear, concise, and consistent sales onboarding program:

- *Will your sales onboarding program prioritize your customer's needs versus your company's products or services?* Design your program to be customer-centric instead of a product, features, and benefits dump. The fastest way to create relevance with customers is to understand their challenges as well as, if not better than, they do. Your onboarding program can establish this knowledge base.

- *Is your sales onboarding program based on mastering sales conversations while listening, talking, and utilizing technology simultaneously?* Your onboarding design can begin with teaching hands-on experiences, like opening a call while updating data in the CRM. From there, the design can build toward mastering complex customer conversations. The lessons should be seamless and interconnected, so that your sales professionals don't forget what they learned earlier in the course. I recommend *against* separating the content related to customers, products, and technology.

- ***Does your sales onboarding program enable a blend of structured and self-paced learning?*** No two people learn at the same pace. With that in mind, it is important that your program accommodates all types of learners (visual, auditory, and kinesthetic). Make sure that your onboarding design allows for a healthy mix of structured, facilitated learning and unstructured, non-facilitated learning so that your newly hired sales professionals don't burn out during their initial onboarding experience.

- ***Does your sales onboarding program include role-specific, on-the-job, and peer mentoring throughout the learning experience?*** Research consistently shows that the impact of a coach or mentor dramatically increases sales performance. After sales professionals learn a core concept, have them listen to and, if possible, participate in sales conversations that will reinforce the concepts they just learned with a coach or mentor. This way your newly hired sales professionals won't graduate from your onboarding program only to be told "forget everything you learned" by veteran sellers once they've integrated into the sales team.

- ***Does your sales onboarding program continue once the course or workshop experience is completed?*** According to behaviorists, learning can be defined as a relatively permanent change in behavior brought about as a result of experience or practice. Until people have truly mastered the fundamentals, they need continued support and reinforcement. Remember, learning is a marathon, not a sprint! Make sure that your onboarding design is the first step in a continuous learning journey.

Role-specific Business Acumen: BDRs and SDRs

Role-specific business acumen is all about getting the right content to the right people, at the right time, in such a way that they can easily consume and implement it. What is too technical for one role may not be technical enough for another. With that in mind, you will want to include role-specific content, tools, and Guided Learning Plans (GLPs) in your sales enablement program design.

Let's focus on the BDR/SDR roles. The primary responsibility of both a BDR (business development representative) and SDR (sales development representative) is to qualify or disqualify leads at the initial stage in the sales cycle. When working with these roles, the bulk of your sales enablement activities should focus on the art and science of sharpening their discovery and qualification skills. This should range from teaching which questions should be a high priority for your company's ICP, to the tools and platforms that can be used to automate and scale the search for contact information.

Keep in mind that the BDR/SDR role is generally the entry point into sales and sometimes even into the corporate environment. Never assume that things are *obvious* unless you want to set your new hires up for failure. Everything they learn will come from a mix of your sales enablement programs and peer learning experiences. Your programs must be clear, concise, and consistent. This often means that instead of 30 or 60 minute modules, you share what I call *knowledge bites*. These are short three to five minute assets, podcasts, presentations, or webinar clips focused on the BDR/SDR roles, including sales best practices, tool deployment, or examples of failures to avoid.

Here are a few components that I have seen work successfully when onboarding BDRs and SDRs.

- **Academic Approaches:** This is usually their first or second job after completing their college degree, and they're accustomed to structure, predictability, and a consistent syllabus. I recommend following a similar process within your sales enablement onboarding design.

- **Teach That Sales Is a Numbers Game:** At the end of the day, sales is a numbers game. You are either above or below your quota target. It is your job to teach sales professionals how to successfully approach prospects and grow from every meeting or conversation. As the old adage goes, "With competence comes confidence!"

- Remember They're Newbies: The faster that they feel comfortable with the onboarding process, the faster they will assimilate into your company's culture and immerse themselves in the onboarding content. This means that your content should start at a fundamental level and progressively work toward the key components of doing the job in the real world. And stay away from industry-specific acronyms! The goal is to provide a baseline of knowledge, not have them run to Google every 15 minutes.

- Encourage a Proactive Attitude: As one of my mentors, Tom Mendoza, chairman of NetApp, shared repetitively, "The only thing we expect from BDRs and SDRs is a positive attitude and a willingness to learn, because the only thing you can control is your attitude." It's your job as a sales enablement practitioner to foster both of those qualities. For many new hires, this is one of the scariest experiences of their lives, and it is often the first time they're acting as an adult without a safety net. This is your opportunity to articulate what is now expected of them. You can stress and clearly articulate that they must take an active role in achieving success in their careers. One of my favorite statements when meeting with BDRs and SDRs is, "You must own the direction of your own career. No executive or manager has more vested interest in it than you do."

- **Focus on the Basics:** My recommendation is to ease BDRs and SDRs into this transition slowly, by focusing initially on the basics of integrating into the company. What exactly do I mean by the basics? While this could cover a wide spectrum of things, I will narrow it down to four basic proven strategies that I have shared with every BDR and SDR I have ever mentored.

1. Talk less, listen more.

2. Be curious and *genuine.* No one has time for fluff, and we all know when someone is being insincere.

3. Teach about qualifying in as well as out. While a successful discovery and qualification call makes you feel good, it is equally important to qualify a prospect out of the sales cycle. Not every prospect will fit your ICP. The second best answer you can hear from a prospect or customer is no. Sometimes this is where the sales cycle really begins!

4. Don't be afraid to say *I don't know.* No one expects you to have all of the answers right away. The best way to learn is to ask questions and maintain a positive attitude. It's amazing how many opportunities this will create for you.

In general, the mark of a successful onboarding program is when your learners gain enough exposure to real-life selling experience that they develop enough confidence to step into their new role prepared to show their value. Always keep in mind that the sales onboarding experience will not only establish their baseline of success within your company, but will also set the bar for the ongoing learning journey that I will discuss further in the following two chapters.

Above all else, it is critical that your training and onboarding programs are aligned with the company's sales leaders. Sales professionals should view both organizations as a single, cohesive unit working collaboratively and cross-functionally to drive increased revenue and seller productivity. Sales enablement can create the most effective, world-class enablement processes, programs, and platforms, but if the adoption, execution, and modeling of positive behavior is not owned by the sales leader, it will never be utilized.

No good general wants to lead their troops into war without the proper level of preparation or tools. Training without an iterative enablement strategy is like leading your sellers to war with no plan and a plastic spoon. As the old adage goes, "What is important to your leader is imperative to you!" Always remember that the most direct route to ongoing success lies with the successful partnership between your sales enablement organization and sales leaders.

PART 3: Creating Long-Term Success

Chapter 9

THE VALUE OF SALES LEADERSHIP COACHING

PEOPLE ARE INFLUENCED TO CHANGE BY PEOPLE THEY TRUST
—*Mike Bosworth*

Some of my biggest heroes are the amazing hall of fame athletes. They have a specific set of skills that allow them to far excel above and beyond their competition. Unfortunately, some of them also became the worst coaches in the history of their given sport. Why were they so bad at coaching after excelling in the elite category as players?

It's simple: they had no idea how to translate their reasons for being successful as an individual contributor into a scalable and repeatable process as a coach. Now let me relate this to the sales environment in most companies. I don't think that most sales managers believe that they're inept as coaches. Yet the truth is, some of them are. The issue is that most have no idea how to coach and little past experience with coaching.

It's one of your core jobs as a sales enablement practitioner to harness the best practices from successful leaders and work with each of them to articulate and document best practices. Once you have that documentation, it becomes possible to use the best practices as a coaching tool and deploy them as scalable and repeatable processes across your company's sales organization.

Creating Effective Sales Coaches

Coaching to me is one of the most overused and misunderstood phrases in Corporate America. Unfortunately, the definition has become synonymous with, "I have knowledge that you need so this is my opportunity to tell you how to fix your problem." In fact, coaching should be the opposite of telling someone what they should do. A true coach is a great listener. Their focus should be on *why* something was said as opposed to *what* was said and how it should be messaged or positioned differently.

The definition of sales coaching is a process followed by sales managers to maximize a sales professional's performance, allowing them to positively impact the greater sales team. The process is designed so that every sales professional is supported and coached to effectively contribute to the team's ability to reach, or exceed, quota.

The Importance of Reinforcement: It is critical that we are continuously sharpening the skillset of sales professionals and sales leaders. With that in mind, leaders should always be involved in the initial onboarding process, as I discussed in chapter 8. Onboarding must always be viewed within the larger context of a company's ability to **reinforce** the learning baseline that has been established. This is all about continuous improvement to ensure practical application of what has been learned. As I've mentioned before, "you train animals and you enable people." Anyone can be trained to do a task once and walk away; the art and science comes in when you provide a road map that allows the initial training to continually iterate. And coaching is an important part of that iteration.

The need for reinforcement will change as your company's go-to-market strategy shifts, competitive landscape expands, and product or service offerings shift. While sales enablement is responsible for the framework, strategy, measurements, and metrics, the reinforcement process can't be owned by the sales enablement organization. This must be owned, adopted, and modeled by the first- and second-line managers (FLMs). They are truly where the rubber meets the road. We can provide them with the most efficient, well-tuned programs, but if FLMs don't model it on a daily basis, the reinforcement strategy will die a slow and painful death.

One of the most common mistakes I have seen in my career is when sales enablement neglects the importance of teaching sales leaders to prepare and coach their teams. Too many times we as sales enablement practitioners have assumed that sales leaders have all of the knowledge required to be a good coach, or that they will take the time to up-level their coaching skills. The longer I have spent as a sales enablement practitioner, the more I have realized this is usually the furthest thing from the truth.

- ***The Importance of Sales Performance Management:*** The joint goal of the sales leader and sales enablement practitioner is to improve the sales proficiency of sales professionals, which will lead to an increase in productivity. The coaching activities of sales leaders should always be oriented toward these larger goals, and the most efficient way to achieve them is through a consistent pipeline management strategy.

- The purpose of sales performance management is to boost employee engagement and productivity. The established belief is that engaged employees stay longer, actively involve themselves in the workplace, and produce better results. Pipeline management is not a newly established concept. All sales professionals need an effective way to manage their pipeline. The question becomes, are they managing the pipeline as effectively as possible? As an example, even though a sales professional may be hitting their quota goals and gaining new customers, they may not be as effective when it comes to upselling or finding new opportunities with existing customers.

- While pipeline management is extremely important, most great sales professionals must be continually reminded of how and why this will make them more efficient and effective. It's not that they don't want to do a great job around pipeline management, it's that they're not typically admin-intensive by nature. And for the most part, these great sellers just want to *sell*—most believe that all the other stuff will fall into place.

- We as leaders and sales enablement practitioners should focus on teaching sales professionals that the definition of success *is not just about selling*. It's more about how to ensure we have a strategy for how we do things, including how we manage the pipeline and how we determine what is the most effective way to increase revenue attainment while simultaneously creating a better customer experience.

Coaching Sales Leaders: As sales enablement professionals, we're not only working with sales leaders on their techniques for coaching sales professionals. We're also coaching the sales leaders themselves. Here is some advice that I received early in my sales enablement career from the best sales leader I have ever partnered with:

> The net worth of any sales leader is their belief that their team is successful based upon their coaching advice, previous experience, and drive to succeed. If you want to gain the respect and support of a sales leader, you must show them *why* they need to change the way that they're doing things today, not just *how* the change will yield different and sometimes stronger results.

That simple advice has not only served me well but taught me that most sales leaders will continue doing things the way they have always done them unless they're shown *why* doing things differently will make their lives easier and more productive. Your job as a sales enablement practitioner is to find a delicate (okay, sometimes not-so-delicate) way to show the *why* versus the *what* or *how* when it comes to the value of coaching.

- When a sales leader asks for coaching, what they're really saying is, "Please let me know if what I'm saying or doing is the *best* way to do it, or if you have seen or experienced a different way." If you answer a sales leader's question with a series of questions, they sometimes come to a conclusion on their own, because the questioning process allows them to draw upon their own experiences to solve their problems. And if they can't solve the problem, they now feel empowered to ask you for help, because your question-oriented approach has created a safe environment that encourages two-way communication. More importantly, it shows the sales leader that you have their best interest and personal growth in mind, which in turn will help to build an enormous amount of credibility between you and them.

- Most sales leaders aren't looking to be told what or how to do something. They're usually looking for validation that they have covered all of their bases. According to Tamera Schmidt, founder and CEO of Enlightened Coach, "A coach is best defined as a leader who inspires growth through experimental leadership."

- The next time a sales leader asks you for coaching, remember that this is a pivotal moment in your sales enablement career that will have a longstanding impact. Stop for a moment, take a deep breath, then confidently ask if they want you to *listen, coach,* or *fix* before you give them your thoughts or feedback.

In general I have found that the most effective way to get to know a sales leader and their business is to show genuine, authentic interest in them and why they do the job that they do. The best way to disarm a sales leader is to ask questions about them. Warning, please schedule a good chunk of time in this meeting and be prepared to hear a few war stories!

Leading with Sales EQ

This discussion about coaching is the perfect juncture to talk about sales IQ versus EQ. Erika Granath defines sales IQ as a "wide range of technologies that help salespeople find, monitor, and understand information on prospect's and existing client's daily business." While sales IQ has always been required to understand your buyers, build rapport, and close deals, emotional intelligence (EQ) is equally as important to ensure that we are creating more sales leaders and fewer followers.

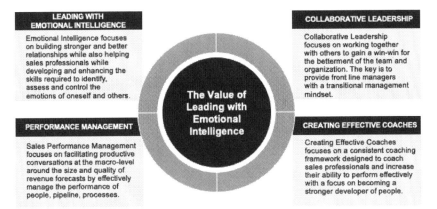

LEADING WITH EMOTIONAL INTELLIGENCE

Emotional Intelligence focuses on building stronger and better relationships while also helping sales professionals while developing and enhancing the skills required to identify, assess and control the emotions of oneself and others.

PERFORMANCE MANAGEMENT

Sales Performance Management focuses on facilitating productive conversations at the macro-level around the size and quality of revenue forecasts by effectively manage the performance of people, pipeline, processes.

The Value of Leading with Emotional Intelligence

COLLABORATIVE LEADERSHIP

Collaborative Leadership focuses on working together with others to gain a win-win for the betterment of the team and organization. The key is to provide front line managers with a transitional management mindset.

CREATING EFFECTIVE COACHES

Creating Effective Coaches focuses on a consistent coaching framework designed to coach sales professionals and increase their ability to perform effectively with a focus on becoming a stronger developer of people.

Figure 8: The Importance of Sales Leaders

One of the biggest mistakes I have seen throughout my career is that most sales enablement practitioners are so focused on enabling sales professionals that they completely overlook the needs of sales leaders. Just like sales professionals, it's important for your sales leaders to continually evolve and sharpen their leadership skills. The best way to allow this to happen is to incorporate a sales leadership coaching process in your overall program design—and to ensure that the importance of EQ is a big part of that program.

There has never been a time where leading with humanity, empathy, and emotional intelligence has meant more than it does today. Traditionally, sales managers are mostly focused on closing sales and exceeding quota, but times have shifted. Just as the buyer's journey, sales success metrics, and sales processes have changed, it's time for sales managers to embrace the role of becoming sales leaders. In order to be successful in this role, a sales leader must balance being a part-time motivator, part-time mentor, and part-time counselor. This all has to be achieved while simultaneously ensuring that their teams never lose sight of the goal of closing sales and creating satisfied customers. It's no small feat!

As a sales enablement practitioner, your sales coaching program must provide balance in the areas of thinking, feeling, and behavior by giving leaders the essential skills and mindset needed for proper self-awareness. Leading with emotional intelligence should then translate into sales coaches who will adjust their style of feedback and corrective action conversations with each member of their team rather than taking a one-size-fits-all approach. This will also serve as a modeling mechanism for sales professionals around how to coach versus simply being an inflexible manager. It's a proven fact that most sales professionals will do what they see their sales leaders do more often than what they're being *told* is the right way to do things.

With that in mind, it's essential to teach sales leaders the importance of **collaborative leadership**, the key word here being *collaborative*. Experienced sales leaders often rely on their previous experiences—both positive and negative—to lead their teams. They will continue to rely upon these experiences until they're shown why they should coach versus manage their team. Your sales coaching program should offer first-line managers the transitional elements needed to move from an individual contributor to a sales leadership mindset. This means sales leaders should focus on *modeling* the right behaviors that will drive increased results across their entire sales team.

Modeling positive behavior also extends to the tone and tenor of each meeting, not just the content. I believe that the proper tone and tenor can be established if the sales leader asks a simple, three-part question at the beginning of every 1:1 meeting with sales professionals. This is the same question that I previously mentioned, and it comes in handy within a variety of contexts:

Do you want me to listen, coach, or fix?

This is a critical question because most sales leaders are natural fixers. That is what got them to this level of their career. But sometimes a fix isn't what's needed in a given situation. It could be that the sales professional simply needs to hear their thoughts and sales approach outside of their heads. Sometimes it could be that the sales professional is encountering a situation or objection for the first time. Finally, it could also be that the sales professional has exhausted all approaches and is looking to their sales leader for guidance, direction, and wisdom. The goal of this question is that it will allow the sales leader to put on the right set of ears for the conversation rather than immediately going into *fix* mode. It also shows the sales professional that the meeting is completely focused on them.

The tips and techniques for effective coaching discussed in this chapter will be supported if the wider company embraces a culture of learning. Let's take a look at this more deeply in the next chapter.

Chapter 10

BUILDING A CULTURE OF LEARNING

IF CULTURE CHANGES, EVERYTHING CHANGES.
—*Michael Fullan*

Building a Culture of Learning seems to be on all of the sales enablement bingo cards these days, but what does it really mean? As I mentioned earlier, learning is more like a marathon than a sprint. Building a culture of learning is an iterative process rather than a one-time occurrence, and you must secure participation and buy-in from leaders and organizations across the company.

It all begins with having a comprehensive sales enablement charter that covers strategy, architecture, and execution, as discussed in chapter 5. It means that you have established strong lines of communication with executive sponsors, and it includes personal and professional development programs, learning reinforcement strategies, and plans that strategically align technology resources and revenue-generating metrics.

Above all, building a culture of learning is about the ability to listen, an openness to learn from others, and a strong collaboration and sense of trust between enablement and sales leaders and professionals.

I remember the exact moment I realized I had been given the opportunity to learn the *secret handshake* of sales. I was working for Network Appliance, a data storage company in Silicon Valley, as a sales training manager. As with all hyper-growth companies, we were struggling with how to increase revenue without impacting the incredible culture that had been crafted by the executive leadership team. During our sales boot camp postmortem meetings, the VP of Sales posed a question that I had never been asked before: "How can we build a world-class sales team that will not only drive increased revenue, but also be the kind of people who our customers will trust?"

My response was, "You have to work with your leaders to hire the type of people who you would trust if you were a prospect or a customer." He smiled and winked. It was at that moment that I knew I had officially received the honor of the Network Appliance sales secret handshake!

If you want to build a culture of learning, it's essential to first build rapport and trust with your sales organization. This is all about gaining credibility, and making clear that you're willing to listen to sales leaders' ideas rather than enforcing YOUR assumption about the solutions. One way to quickly gain credibility is to schedule a meeting with each of your senior sales leaders and ask them the following 10 questions:

1. What is your definition of sales enablement?

2. If you had a blank canvas, what would you see as the top 3-5 priorities for this quarter and fiscal year for your team(s)?

3. What is your definition of success, beyond "hitting the number"?

4. How long is it currently taking to successfully onboard a new sales professional?

5. How are you currently tracking and reporting on the components of their onboarding experience?

6. What type of feedback are you receiving around their onboarding experience?

7. Who are your most successful first-line managers (FLMs) and sales professionals, so that I can get their input and feedback?

8. What if I could create a way to scale your top performers and drive more incremental revenue at a faster rate?

9. What are you willing to commit to in order to ensure the success of your FLMs and their direct reports?

10. How soon can we meet again so that I can share the results with you?

These questions will give you a sales-focused foundation for your programs. Once you have the answers to these questions, the real work begins. You need to analyze the feedback, create a baseline strategy, and circle back with your internal customers to confirm that you heard what they were saying, and that you interpreted it correctly.

Once you have established this baseline relationship and start to build trust, the next step is to establish credibility. A great place to start is by speaking in *sales speak*. Let me repeat this: *A great place to start is by speaking in sales speak*. Similar to the secret handshake that I mentioned, the sales organization has a language that only they speak and understand. Do **NOT** attempt to transform them into speaking sales enablement jargon. They have no want, need, or desire to learn a new language. That is the shortest route to damaging the relationship that you have worked so diligently at building.

Gaining and Leveraging Cross-functional Executive Sponsorship

According to Heller Consulting, change does not come easily to most organizations. Inertia often rules the day, and Newton's First Law of Motion—a body at rest remains at rest—can prove difficult to overcome. In fact, there is a fundamental difference between simply wanting something new and actually being open and willing to change. Even strong advocates for a new system have been known to try recreating their old, inefficient, or outdated processes within the new system.

As a sales enablement practitioner, it's important to help create a culture of openness to change rather than a culture of inertia. This is where strong executive sponsorship can make a significant difference. The executive sponsor is the leader tasked with ensuring that stakeholders throughout the organization are engaged and understand the following:

- Why the sales enablement initiative is being undertaken and how the change will impact the organization

- Which individuals are involved, and how they will be participating in the engagement and helping to move the organization forward

- The organizational vision and the project's goals, and how they will impact staff and other internal and external constituents

- The benefits that will come from embracing the change

Without this level of support, assistance, and sponsorship, your sales enablement programs will never get off the ground, let alone have the level of impact on the sales organization and company that you're shooting for.

In order to successfully gain and leverage cross-functional executive support you will need to navigate the following three strategies:

1. Articulate the value of your program

2. Design and deploy a process that focuses on driving executive-level sponsorship and iterative feedback

3. Deliver a clear, concise, and collaborative executive communication plan

You might be wondering what to include when articulating the value of your organization, team, and programs. The first step in the process is the creation of a project overview that outlines the value of the program's outcomes and metrics. You will want to spend most of your time creating and vetting the program overview component. This should serve as a road map for anyone interested in understanding all of your sales enablement programs at a glance. It should include things like who needs to be engaged, why it is critical to success, how it aligns to the company's goals, a detailed list of your program deliverables, metrics, and KPIs, pilot delivery strategy, and of course an implementation and reinforcement plan.

While the key components are important, the crafting of consistent messaging and positioning is where I have seen the process either accelerate or fail. As we all know, sometimes it's not about *what* is said and more about *how* it is said. With that in mind, always ensure that your messaging and positioning statements are in the words of your internal customers, *not sales enablement jargon*.

Your messaging should also be vetted and approved across multiple internal customers at multiple levels. Focus on how this will increase customer satisfaction, decrease time to revenue, cut costs, mitigate risk, and increase sales productivity. Next, ask for their best practices, input, and assistance, not just a confirmation of your plan. *It is critical that the executive sponsor understands that their input is not only needed but valued.*

In order to gain the necessary level of executive sponsorship, you must deliver a clear, concise, and collaborative executive communication plan. I remember meeting with a chief revenue officer early in my career to discuss adding additional headcount to my growing sales enablement team. During the meeting we covered the usual questions and I outlined the metrics I was using to justify the additional headcount. After a few minutes focused on statistics and metrics, he asked the central question that shifted the direction of the meeting: "How will increasing the size of your sales enablement team help my sales organization hit quota faster?"

This is the very question I had prepared for! From that point forward, our meeting was more focused on how the additional team members would directly meet the needs of his sales teams.

While I didn't walk out of that meeting with a promise of additional headcount, this laid the groundwork, and ultimately budget was allocated for two additional team members who were added the following quarter.

There are several key components that should be included in an executive communication plan. It all begins with clearly articulating the value and components of your plan. Sales productivity and growth can only be attained by having an intentional plan backed by years of experience and specific components required to deliver the desired results. Creating scalable and repeatable processes as well as templates will help you to generate a pattern of success. You should not create a process that needs to be redesigned every time there's a new problem! Instead, you can create a single process that can be iterated to address multiple problems. As you grow in your role as a sales enablement practitioner, you will learn that the copy and paste function was designed with us in mind!

Attaining enthusiastic buy-in from executive sponsors is an important part of building a culture of learning. Another component is deepening your level of communication and collaboration with sales leaders and senior leaders throughout the company. Let's take a look at some of the particular topics you should always emphasize when speaking with leadership. This is an important part of building trust and credibility. They are best practices I have used to successfully communicate my sales enablement strategy to senior leaders in a way that led to an increase in the level of respect for my sales enablement teams:

1. Ensure that your enablement strategy is tied directly to the company's top initiatives.

2. Work with the company and/or sales leadership teams to ensure that sales enablement is publicly supported and driven from the highest points in your organization. This can't be seen as solely a "sales enablement initiative!"

3. Collaborate with your sales leader to help them become your sales enablement marketing machine. They should be responsible for communicating your sales enablement

goals, deliverables, and success. This will lead to sales enablement being woven into the fabric of the company.

4.   Sales enablement must be viewed as a valued partner of the sales organization. This begins by working with and through the first-line managers to drive adoption, execution, and modeling of your programs, processes, and tools.

5.   All of your sales enablement programs, processes, and tools must be communicated in the form of the impact that they have on revenue, not the activities that surround their deployment.

As we explored in chapter 7, sales enablement practitioners are most successful when they're part of an orchestra that spans the many departments and organizations at a company. The beautiful thing about this orchestra is it also creates trust, credibility, and a culture of learning.

Reinforcement: It Separates Training from Sales Enablement

Sales enablement is not always about BIG wins or accomplishments. Most of the time, it's simply about the sum of all of the parts. It's about wins and losses that turned into learning experiences and the development of best practices. While training is a part of enablement, it is a small part that leads to the collective definition. I would even venture to say that training is a one-time occurrence, while enablement is an ongoing and iterative process.

Figure 9: The Value of Sales Enablement Reinforcement

The biggest differentiator between training and enablement is reinforcement. As we explored in chapter 8, onboarding programs lose value when they're not strategically combined with reinforcement strategies. But the importance of reinforcement extends to all aspects of an enablement organization, which is why a larger culture of reinforcement must be baked into multiple layers and processes.

I believe that sales enablement reinforcement comes in three forms and can be used to validate your sales enablement team as revenue influencers. I say influencers rather than revenue drivers because we are not responsible for securing revenue.

> **Adoption & Execution:** The ability to measure adoption and usage of all implemented enablement processes, programs, productivity tools, and templates

> **Seller Readiness:** The ability to determine whether sellers are effectively enabled and ready to maximize their engagements with prospects and customers

> **Metrics & KPIs:** The ability to support validation of tracking and reporting of sales activities and tools related to revenue-generating metrics

Reinforcement is a collaborative process that spans across the entire company. Remember how we talked about enablement being compared to an orchestra? With that analogy in mind, I would compare reinforcement to an encore. It's not the initial act, but it's what ensures that what you have learned can now be put into practical application.

When it comes to determining who owns the reinforcement activities in your company, there are two questions you will need to answer.

- Why is sales reinforcement so important?

- Who owns sales enablement adoption vs execution?

To help define reinforcement's importance, let's think about a sales kickoff event. These events usually include a lot of fun, awards, and the rollout of updated messaging, positioning, and selling motions. What if everyone was excited about the event, but once they left, they forgot all about the information they learned? What if they went back to their office only to learn that everything they learned wasn't reflected in the actual program? The event would have been a waste of time and budget. The same can be said for rolling out a new sales enablement program without a reinforcement plan. Without an iterative strategy, it's just a waste of time and budget.

The sales enablement team should include a reinforcement strategy within every new sales enablement program rollout. Doing this will save you a lot of explanation after the program release, and it ensures that all of your internal customers are aware of the goals, deliverables, and metrics related to the program. It also gives them an opportunity to vet your program prior to its release and include their feedback, suggestions, or recommendations before the program is deployed.

It's amazing how engaged and collaborative your internal customers will be once they feel like they're a part of the overall build and deployment process rather than having it thrust upon them. Asking for feedback early in the process can lead to a lot less hurt feelings, personal confrontations, and complaints from your internal stakeholders later.

The next question that needs to be addressed is who owns the adoption and execution of sales enablement programs. It really comes down to whether your sales enablement team is valued by your sales leadership team. In a best-case scenario, this is a joint ownership between sales leadership, first-line managers (FLMs), and sales enablement. The sales leadership team should set the scope around needs and expectations. The first-line managers should own the modeling of positive behavior that their teams will follow. The sales enablement organization should own the design, deployment tools, metrics, and communications.

The best way I have found to gain support from the FLMs is to share your sales enablement post-event strategy, milestones, deliverables, metrics, and enablement calendar with your sales leaders during the sales kickoff event planning process. This will not only build trust in your plan but give you an opportunity to secure the sales leader's endorsement and ownership of the overall reinforcement strategy. The reinforcement strategy cannot be viewed by your sales leaders as simply a *new* sales enablement plan that might potentially add more deliverables onto their plates.

To ensure the highest level of success, the strategy should be rolled out by your highest-ranking sales leader so that it will be accepted by the FLMs and sales professionals as an initiative that is owned and driven by that sales leader. With this in mind, I highly recommend building and vetting the plan with your highest-ranking leader, then step out of the way and watch the magic of adoption and execution happen!

When it comes to creating *long-term success* as a sales enablement organization, coaching, reinforcement, collaboration, and building a culture of learning are all vital. Another fundamental aspect of long-term success involves the tools that you're using. Let's take a closer look at the tools that are important for any world-class sales enablement organization.

Chapter 11

SALES ENABLEMENT TOOLS

GIVE ORDINARY PEOPLE THE RIGHT TOOLS, AND THEY WILL DESIGN AND BUILD THE MOST EXTRAORDINARY THINGS.
–Neil Gershenfeld

In my 20+ year career, I have come across just about every sales enablement tool, technology, and platform available. Let me put this knowledge to use and help you to *demystify the dark matter* around these tools, technologies, and platforms.

Sales enablement tools have become a critical component that drives success across your company, but it's important to *always* remember that just because a new shiny tool is available does **NOT** mean that it's a fit for where your company is in its maturation cycle. It's important to do your homework before you select a sales enablement tool or platform.

The problem is that selecting, designing, building, implementing, and integrating these tools can be a full-time job within itself. Too many times I have seen sales enablement practitioners get enamored with the latest cool, fun, shiny technology. They get led down a rabbit trail that ultimately pulls them and their teams away from the one true reason that they need the technology. The technology should be used as a means of automating and scaling their ability to service their internal customers.

To give you a sense of the plethora of tools that might be needed, here is an example of a sales enablement tech stack:

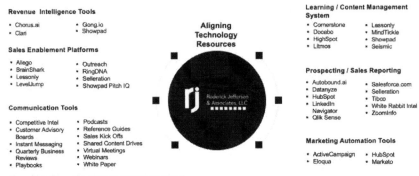

Revenue Intelligence Tools

- Chorus.ai
- Clari
- Gong.io
- Showpad

Sales Enablement Platforms

- Allego
- BrainShark
- Lessonly
- LevelJump
- Outreach
- RingDNA
- Selleration
- Showpad Pitch IQ

Communication Tools

- Competitive Intel
- Customer Advisory Boards
- Instant Messaging
- Quarterly Business Reviews
- Playbooks
- Podcasts
- Reference Guides
- Sales Kick Offs
- Shared Content Drives
- Virtual Meetings
- Webinars
- White Paper

Aligning Technology Resources

Learning / Content Management System

- Cornerstone
- Docebo
- HighSpot
- Litmos
- Lessonly
- MindTickle
- Showpad
- Seismic

Prospecting / Sales Reporting

- Autobound.ai
- Datanyze
- HubSpot
- LinkedIn Navigator
- Qlik Sense
- Salesforce.com
- Selleration
- Tibco
- White Rabbit Intel
- ZoomInfo

Marketing Automation Tools

- ActiveCampaign
- Eloqua
- HubSpot
- Marketo

Figure 10: Building a Sales Enablement Technology Stack

Here is a small word of sage advice: *If it looks too good to be true, it probably is!* As sales enablement practitioners, we gain a sixth sense over time that allows us to cut through the fluff and noise when it comes to selecting new tools and technology. My recommendation is to focus less on the *what* or *how* the technology will be used and put your focus squarely on *why* the technology is needed. I have learned to approach tools and technology more as a way to align technology resources rather than attempting to build a technology stack with individual tools, technologies, and platforms. With this in mind, I have narrowed the selection criteria down to eight categories.

1. Content Management Systems

2. Learning Management Systems

3. Prospecting Tools

4. Sales Reporting Tools

5. Marketing Automation Tools

6. Communication Tools

7. Sales Coaching Tools

8. Revenue Intelligence Platforms

Let's dig a little deeper into each of these categories. Outlined below are some best practices that have served me well throughout my career. Keep in mind that this is not an exhaustive list. It will vary based upon the size and maturation point of your company.

Content and Learning Management Systems

Sales professionals are not admin-intensive by nature and tend to have very short attention spans. This is by no means taking a shot at sales professionals. This is part of what makes them good at their jobs. I say this as someone who used to be one, in addition to my decades of direct interaction with salespeople, as supporting evidence.

If you don't have a single repository, salespeople will not look in multiple places for content or information. Instead they will create their own, and this leads to inconsistent messaging and confusion with your customers. Content management systems provide a single location for all content, decks, documents, customer-facing white papers, case studies, competitive briefs, and product updates. The tool will also ensure that the most current and relevant content is shared at all times. There is nothing worse than mixing new, relevant, updated content with old, antiquated, archaic content.

Retiring Old Content: Old content can be retired by implementing a quarterly content review cycle. There is extremely high value in this exercise. It allows your sales professionals to rank content based upon what is being viewed and downloaded rather than how valuable *you* feel an asset is.

Content reviews are a brilliant way to initiate a conversation with your marketing and product marketing teams on a quarterly basis. I would recommend running a report on the highest and lowest number of times an asset was accessed and downloaded in the previous month. This will allow the sales enablement organizations to remove any conjecture or personal bias when making content decisions. This also drives the sales enablement organization to depend on clear, user-driven data points as the basis of making recommendations around when and why assets should be retired from the content management system.

The need for content retirement is typically related to outdated competitive intelligence information, updated messaging and positioning documents, or new sales enablement documentation. Automated user feedback reporting is a critical component to research when selecting a content management system. I would recommend a 4- to 5-star rating system similar to Amazon's that allows your sales professionals to rate and compare assets.

Selecting a Content Management System: When selecting a content management system, the two most reliable ways that I have utilized are 1) crowd sourcing through my trusted network of sales enablement practitioners, and 2) online research comparison companies like G2.

I recommend beginning with your network because they will provide you with an honest assessment of the pros and cons of a given tool. They have firsthand experience and have tried them out successfully or unsuccessfully. They don't have a horse in the race, and they're in your corner. They can prevent you from enduring some of the hiccups or mistakes that they have encountered. As one of my mentors, Tom Mendoza, chairman of Network Appliance, says, "Never underestimate the power of work that others will do for you!"

The second source is online comparison research. I highly recommend G2.com as a reliable source. This platform allows you to review and select the right software and services for your business based on 1M+ authentic, timely reviews from real users. This means that sales enablement practitioners, just like you, who have implemented a given tool share their unbiased feedback. It's also a great way to pay it forward once you have implemented a new tool, technology, or platform. As the old adage goes, "Each one, teach one." It does truly take a community to make each of us bigger, faster, and stronger.

Learning Management Systems: A Learning Management System (LMS) serves several purposes and provides a baseline of value for your sales enablement organization. It will serve as a single location for all of your sales professional's learning history, assessments, accreditation, and certification scores. It will also serve as a simple, easy-to-follow process that will help to remove the confusion and frustration for your sales professionals that comes from having to search in multiple locations for content, scores, and metrics.

This tool will also provide your sales enablement organization with a way to create Guided Learning Plans (GLPs) as a means of documenting role-specific learning accomplishments. These tools might be very important to your role as a sales enablement practitioner. I can't count the number of times I've had executive-level conversations including the *hows*, *whats*, and *whys* around the implementation of role-specific learning plans through our content management systems.

If you're not aware of the importance of implementing role-specific GLPs, here is a quick explanation of their value. They ensure that the correct level of information gets to the right role, and at the right time, in order to be shared across the buyer's cycle. As I mentioned earlier, what may be considered too technical or complex for one role may not be technical or descriptive enough for another role. What this means in simple terms is that you can create a culture of learning that spans across every component of a sales professional's lifetime, beginning with onboarding, leading into continuous learning, and culminating with reinforcement and metrics.

Prospecting, Sales Reporting, and Marketing Automation Tools

Prospecting Tools: Prospecting is the process of initiating and developing new business by searching for potential customers, clients, or buyers for your products or services. The goal of sales prospecting is to move these people, or prospects, through the sales funnel until they eventually convert into revenue-generating customers. Keep in mind that the primary user of these tools will be Business Development Representatives (BDRs) and Sales Development Representatives (SDRs) with a minimal amount of sales experience. Considering this, prospecting tools should be selected based upon creating the easiest and most efficient way to reach the right person, with the right message, and at the right time, with the goal of generating more quality opportunities.

Sales Reporting Tools: The importance of sales reporting tools cannot be overestimated. They help sales leaders monitor the performance of their sales team, plan effective sales strategies, decide on a sales forecasting process, and most importantly, maintain or reduce the length of the sales cycle. These tools are instrumental in providing critical details that can be used to develop accurate forecasts and marketing plans, guide budget planning, and improve decision-making.

When I worked at salesforce.com, we had a saying: "If it's not in Salesforce, it doesn't exist." Initially I thought this was an arrogant statement designed to show how superior the platform is. But then I started having meetings with each of the global sales leaders. I came to realize that the statement was an articulation of the way the system creates consistent contact, customer, and accounts records that drive consistency in pipeline forecasting. It was this consistency that ultimately drove the successful sales motions that created one of the most successful companies globally.

The goal of a sales report is to provide critical analysis of how the business is tracking in all areas of the organization. These tools provide important views that can guide decision-making and allow business owners and sales leaders with the opportunity to investigate and solve any identified issues.

Once information is gathered and reviewed, conclusions can be drawn and recommendations made. The outcome of the sales reporting metrics should be used to explain why an issue has occurred. The metrics may also identify performance problems and will help clarify the possible courses of action.

Marketing Automation Tools: Purchasing, deploying, and utilizing the correct marketing automation tool is essential. Marketing automation tools are used as a hosted or web-based solution, and no software installation is required by a customer. The value of a marketing automation tool is the ability to streamline sales and marketing organizations by replacing high-touch, repetitive manual processes with automated solutions.

While automating your company's marketing campaigns tends to bring in positive results, it is not meant to replace traditional marketing tools or campaigns. It will not replace your seasonal emails, write content for you, or intervene when you need a human touch from sales or customer service.

Marketing automation really shines when it is used to:

- Deliver messages to website visitors, leads, or customers at critical points before, during, or after the purchasing process

- Provide crucial information to these same individuals

- Automate check-ins, follow-ups, or reminders you might otherwise have to delegate to customer service or sales teams

Communication, Sales Coaching, and Revenue Intelligence Tools

Communication Tools: Communication tools are where the dots connect. It's all about finding the appropriate and most effective tools where vital internal best practices, wins, losses, product updates, go-to-market shifts, or accreditations and certifications can be shared consistently. These tools are also a brilliant way to share external competitive landscape changes, partners and alliances, and mergers and acquisitions updates with your sales professionals by utilizing a tool that will not disrupt their selling motions or create additional selling barriers.

Some of the most common communication tools include: annual and quarterly business reviews, online collaboration tools, white papers, and podcasts. Each of these are used to ensure that internal and external messaging is delivered in a clear, concise, and consistent matter. Remember to create a communication strategy that incorporates a variety of delivery formats that will appeal to the seven most commonly accepted learning styles.

- Auditory

- Intrapersonal

- Kinesthetic

- Reading

- Social

- Visual

- Written

The key is to not over-communicate and not under-communicate. I recommend finding a balance between having the *right* tools to clearly communicate, and not having so many tools that none are viewed by your sales professionals as useful. The tools should allow you to share information in a productive, easy-to-use environment. These tools should be a part of the sales enablement team's survey quarterly process to ensure that you are meeting the needs of your internal customers.

Sales Coaching Tools: Sales coaching tools are some of the most significant in your sales enablement bag. They are also constantly changing and evolving, so it's important to stay on top of them. These tools can range from conversation recordings that can be used during real-time coaching sessions, to video communications that can be used as a way of creating a feeling of being in the same room. Regardless of the delivery vehicle, the intent is the same—to provide your sales leaders with the support, tools, and resources required to create a strong, consistent culture of performance and accountability.

Revenue Intelligence Platforms: Throughout my career I have noticed that people's attention spans continue to shrink. Because of this, it's important that your sales enablement organization utilizes what I call *knowledge bites*. These are five- to seven-minute pieces of content in writing, visual, and podcast form that can succinctly enable your sales professionals on a single topic.

Gone are the days of sitting in front of a computer screen and learning by watching 30- to 60-minute voiceover PowerPoint presentations. As technology becomes more advanced and we move toward a remote workforce environment, it is critical that you provide a tool that allows your sales professionals to access information whenever and wherever. This is where revenue intelligence tools like podcast libraries and playlists come in. These tools are so versatile and can be used across the full spectrum of a sales professional's career.

The thing to remember is that while these are short bursts of information, you will want to follow a consistent format when conveying information in this delivery tool. This can include onboarding best practice shares, product updates, competitive intelligence changes, go-to-market shifts, partner and alliance updates, and 1:1 coaching sessions, just to name a few.

What I have seen work effectively is to begin with *What do I want the learner to think?* Follow this up with *What do I want the learner to feel?* Finally, ALWAYS leave them with a call to action, meaning, *What do I want them to adjust or do differently?* This ensures that you are consistently hitting on the points that will resonate with your sales professionals while guiding their learning experience.

★

The key question is how to strategically integrate all of these tools in a way that creates value for your sales professionals and accelerates speed-to-revenue, increases sales productivity, and minimizes barriers to closing deals. You must align all of your sales enablement organization's technology resources to the needs of your sales professionals, prospects, and customers to scale, automate, and drive engagement. You do not need to use every tool just because it is available, but you should find the right tools and use them in the right way.

Here are some of my best practices to keep in mind when researching new sales enablement technology:

Assess and vet new tools: Just because you can, doesn't mean that you should or that it's a good fit for your company. You don't need to integrate all of the shiny new technologies and tools that come your way.

Each purchase should serve a purpose: If the tool will not accelerate speed-to-revenue, increase seller productivity, and create customers for life, it's just a waste of time and resources.

Involve the IT Team: Always work with your information technology team to confirm whether or not a proposed tool will fit into your company's secure technology stack prior to purchasing.

Whether you're selecting a sales coaching tool, a prospecting tool, or a communication tool, never lose sight of *why* you're making the purchase. If the *why* remains your guide, you're less likely to be allured by shiny new products and more likely to find the tool that truly fits your enablement organization's needs.

Chapter 12

METRICS ARE MORE THAN A BUNCH OF NUMBERS

NEVER ASSUME THAT JUST BECAUSE YOU'RE BUSY, YOUR INTERNAL CUSTOMERS VALUE IT AS PRODUCTIVITY. WITHOUT CONTEXT AND METRICS, THEY MAY JUST SEE BUSY-NESS!

You have now learned how to build, deploy, and iterate your sales enablement programs. I would be remiss if I didn't explain how to measure them.

I believe that there are two types of metrics. One set focuses on the things that sales enablement practitioners can *influence*. The other is a set of metrics that sales enablement practitioners *own*. While they're both vitally important, they serve very different purposes. In this chapter, I will show you what it takes to be viewed as an integral part of the sales process by working with sales leaders to determine which metrics to focus on based upon role, responsibility, and sales deliverables.

Let's take a closer look at each of these sets of metrics.

Enablement-Influenced and Enablement-Owned Metrics

Enablement-influenced metrics: As a sales enablement practitioner, you don't actually sell, but your organization is tied to the success or failure of every sales professional and sales leader in your company. Outlined below are some of the most common metrics that will be used to validate or invalidate the value and potentially even the existence of your sales enablement organization in the minds of your company and sales leadership team. I would highly recommend that you work with your sales leadership to define the metrics that are of highest value to them.

- Average Deal size

- Collateral Use and Frequency

- Deal Velocity

- New Pipeline Created

- Number of Closed Deals

- Product Mix by Segment

- Quarter over Quarter

- Annual Quota Attainment Percentage

- Speed to Revenue

- Win and Loss Rates

Return on Investment (ROI): There was a time when sales enablement practitioners could depend on vanity statistics to justify our impact on revenue generation. I call these *smiley sheets* and *butts in seats*! With the increase in budget and resources being allocated to building, sustaining, and growing sales enablement organizations, there is now a need to clearly articulate revenue-impacting metrics to justify these resources. Make no mistake, these metrics are *all* about validation. The following questions help to validate the investment the company has made in building and supporting your sales enablement organization.

- How much impact does the sales enablement organization have on increasing revenue?

- Is the sales enablement organization preparing our sellers to close deals faster?

- Is the sales enablement organization preparing our sales leaders to create more leaders and fewer followers?

- Has the sales enablement organization implemented scalable and repeatable processes, programs, and tools?

- How is sales enablement harnessing the proven best practices or tribal knowledge of our legacy sales professionals and sharing it across the sales organization?

- How would an increase or decrease in headcount across the sales enablement organization impact the attainment of your company's revenue targets?

Enablement-Owned Metrics: These metrics are all about showing the value tied to the outcomes of your sales enablement programs. Here are examples of the types of metrics that sales enablement owns:

- Accreditation and Certification Scores

- Bi-Annual Needs Analysis

- Program-Based Surveys

- Communications Deployed

- eLearning Statistics

- Percentage of Completed Enablement Requests

- Content Usage Statistics

In addition to the enablement-owned metric listed above, there are a number of questions you will need to ask—some of them in conversation with your sales leadership—in order to validate the value of your sales enablement organization. These include:

- Are your sales professionals prepared to show the value of your company's products, solutions, services, and experiences that can only happen by partnering together to prospects and customers?

- Are your sales professionals more productive and efficient because of the processes, programs, and tools being deployed by the sales enablement organization?

- Are your internal business units more aligned and productive because of the influence and actions of the sales enablement organization?

- Are your sales professionals able to consistently message and position enablement's products and services in a way that will create long-term relationships with our company above our competitors?

- Is the sales enablement organization aligned with your company goals and deliverables?

- Is the sales enablement organization proactively soliciting feedback from the sales organization?

- Is the sales enablement team proactively providing feedback and updates regarding their program goals, objectives, and outcomes?

- Is the sales enablement organization consistently providing the leadership team with clear, concise, and revenue-impacting usage statistics and metrics?

It has been said that people can make numbers say anything with the right packaging, angle, messaging, and positioning. But that's not really the case with sales metrics and measurements. It's one of the things I love most about sales and sales enablement. It is cut and dry; either you hit the revenue target, exceed expectations, or fail to accomplish the agreed-upon outcome. At the end of the day, it's not about *what* you measure, but *how* each of these metrics will tie back to the sales enablement organization's impact on the company's deliverables, revenue goals, and customer satisfaction rates.

How Will Artificial Intelligence Impact Sales Enablement?

There was a time not so long ago that metrics analysis was entirely in the hands of humans. Today, AI has been brought on board to help with some of these tasks. How will we use sales enablement tools to scale and automate beyond anything we previously though possible? Let's talk about what gets me really excited: the future of sales enablement!

Growing up as a child, my favorite Saturday morning cartoon was *The Jetsons*. The cartoon shared a futuristic glimpse into how the world would operate in the year 2062. There were self-driving cars that flew around in an orderly and uniform manner above the tallest of skyscraping buildings. There was a robot maid ensuring that the Jetsons' home was immaculately clean at all times. In place of phone calls, all of their conversations were facilitated remotely using television screens. While this all seemed not only unbelievable but unrealistic at the time, some of these far-fetched inventions are considered to be commonplace today.

Sure, we still have not mastered the art and science of flying cars, but we're utilizing artificial intelligence (AI) in autonomous cars today. Communication tools like Zoom that provide remote meeting spaces and classrooms are now a staple of life. Not only has AI changed the way that we live and play, it has also shifted the way that sales enablement organizations are onboarding and educating sales professionals.

While technology like machine learning has been around for decades, AI is only being used by some of the world's most innovative sales enablement organizations. I believe that within the next five years, AI will become a key part of every sales enablement organization, process, and program. This will include AI assistance with deploying and measuring gap analysis, designing and deploying programs, pulling deep sales insights and metrics, and automating the deployment of technology stacks.

★

The start has been slow, but AI has certainly found its way into the sales enablement ecosystem. One example is measurements and metrics. Early in my career it would take days to sort and tabulate assessment scores and program feedback. Thanks to artificial intelligence, these same tasks can be done in a matter of hours and in some cases minutes.

Some of the recent developments in AI have revolved around the ability to recognize and interpret human languages. This began in 2011 with IBM's creation of a question-answering computer system called Watson capable of answering questions posed in natural language. This was developed within IBM's DeepQA project and led by principal investigator David Ferrucci. While this computer system was not created specifically with sales enablement in mind, we have certainly reaped some of the benefits.

One example from my own consulting career is AI's ability to sift through and organize assessments. Each of my company's consulting engagements begins with an assessment that includes feedback from the leadership team, business units, and individual contributors. The goal of this assessment is to uncover the consistent as well as inconsistent feedback from a common set of questions between each of these groups. As you would imagine, it could take days, or even weeks, as well as multiple resource hours to review, index, and format these responses.

This is where AI comes in. We are now able to enter the raw feedback data into an AI tool that automates the process of reviewing, indexing, and formatting the answers, as well as providing a readout that includes keywords and response themes. Imagine how this process has saved many resource hours, not to mention frustration, for my team. This tool has already proven itself to be a productivity tool, and I believe we are just beginning to understand the power that artificial intelligence holds.

I believe that the use of AI will become deeply ingrained in the sales enablement process in the future. It will go well beyond simply calculating and producing metrics. The key to greater productivity is to work smarter, not harder. Working smarter saves precious time and energy and it allows us to focus on the things that really matter.

Here are some statistics suggesting that artificial intelligence will continue to play a significant role and will actually increase over time.

- 83% of CEOs expect the role of AI, machine learning (ML), and robotics to increase significantly in 2021

- 41% of companies are already implementing automation across multiple functions

- 24% of people believe that AI will cause some jobs to go away, yet 83% believe that AI will cause a demand for new skills or jobs being created

The successful integration of AI will depend upon how we utilize and humanize the tool. While programs, processes, and platforms are essential to success, at its core, sales enablement has been, is, and will continue to be all about people. One of our challenges moving forward will be finding a balance between the human element of building rapport, establishing relationships, leading with compassion, and utilizing artificial intelligence. AI is a great way to scale and automate some of the mundane tasks that take sales enablement practitioners away from what we truly love, educating sales professionals.

For those of you who are afraid of exploring or deploying artificial intelligence in your processes and programs, do not let fear, uncertainty, and doubt be the enemy of progress. If you're not using some form of artificial intelligence today in your sales enablement organization, you're already behind the technology curve and most likely working harder, not smarter!

CONNECTING ALL THE DOTS

YOU CAN'T CONNECT THE DOTS LOOKING FORWARD; YOU CAN ONLY CONNECT THEM LOOKING BACKWARDS. SO YOU HAVE TO TRUST THAT THE DOTS WILL SOMEHOW CONNECT IN YOUR FUTURE. YOU HAVE TO TRUST IN SOMETHING—YOUR GUT, DESTINY, LIFE, KARMA, WHATEVER. THIS APPROACH HAS NEVER LET ME DOWN, AND IT HAS MADE ALL THE DIFFERENCE IN MY LIFE.

—*Steve Jobs*

Sales enablement can be challenging in the best of times. The challenges of navigating as a sales enablement practitioner will continue to evolve as the business landscape evolves, and many of the things that were once considered innovative technology will quickly become obsolete. As the business landscape continues to change, it will be up to you as a sales enablement practitioner to define the *next* normal for your people, processes, and programs.

While this can be stressful, new and innovative technologies will emerge that will provide you with an opportunity to re-evaluate and re-invent as well as establish new ways to communicate, collaborate, and orchestrate in ways never thought imaginable with your teams, prospects, and clients. Learning in a virtual environment has become today's new normal. It has created an urgent need for increased structure, cadence, and consistent tools for a company's remote workforce.

We are all in this together! How many times have you heard this from people inside your company? You hear it a lot because it's true, and it reminds me again of the 5 Ps: The most important P will always be *people.*

I would like to share the top 10 sales enablement best practices that have been my guiding light. If you keep these best practices in mind, they will lead to success at your sales enablement organization.

1. We are all on the same team. When one wins, we all win.

2. Sales enablement provides scalable, consistent tools and processes across the lifecycle of a sale.

3. We bring value as change management agents, whether this is at the local, national, international, or leadership levels.

4. Our number one focus is driving incremental revenue.

5. We work collaboratively with sales leaders to help craft the definition of sales success.

6. As part of this collaboration, we are included in the sales interview process.

7. We are laser-focused on accelerating speed-to-revenue.

8. We utilize input and feedback from sellers, leaders, and internal customers, early and often.

9. We consistently use metrics, tracking, and reporting to substantiate Return on Invest (ROI).

10. We work with sales leaders to own the adoption, execution, and modeling of our tools, processes, and programs.

This book has given you a foundation, strategy, and execution plan to assess, build, iterate, measure, and deploy a series of world-class programs, processes, tools, and best practices across your company. As you have learned from reading this book, training is merely a component of sales enablement, and it's not any more or less important than any of the other pieces.

I will leave you with this to ponder. There are those who will embrace the framework of sales enablement 3.0 and thrive by building innovative, cutting-edge, successful sales enablement programs. There are others who will risk failure by continuing to do things as they have always been done. At our core, sales enablement practitioners are *change managements agents*. If you're not anticipating, reacting to, and embracing change, then it will be difficult, if not impossible, to succeed as a sales enablement practitioner.

Sales enablement is not about reacting to what has happened. It is about implementing a proactive approach and systematic strategy that leads to increased sales productivity and increased revenue. If you're up for the challenge of being a visionary sales enablement practitioner in what will become the *next normal*, let me be the first to welcome you to the sales enablement 3.0 era!

ENDNOTES

Chapter 1: Footnote: https://www.saleshacker.com/
what-is-sales-enablement/

Chapter 1: FOOTNOTE: Harvard Business Review

Chapter 1: BUYING CYCLE FOOTNOTE: https://www.
millerheimangroup.com/resources/news/study-half-of-b2b-
buyers-make-up-their-minds-before-talking-to-sales-reps/

Chapter 1: BUYING CYCLE FOOTNOTE: https://www.
bluecorona.com/blog/b2b-marketing-statistics/

Chapter 1: FOOTNOTE: Jeff Davis, Create Togetherness book

Chapter 5: BUYER'S JOURNEY FOOTNOTE: https://www.
fiind.com/blog/buyers-journey-get-better-results/

Chapter 5: BUYER'S JOURNEY IMPLEMENTATION
FOOTNOTE:
https://www.salesforce.com/blog/customer-service-stats/

Chapter 7: WHAT IS SALES INTELLIGENCE FOOTNOTE:

https://www.vainu.com/blog/best-sales-intelligence-tools/

Chapter 10: EXECUTIVE SPONSORSHIP
FOOTNOTE: https://teamheller.com/resources/blog/
the-importance-of-executive-sponsorship

Chapter 12: PROSPECTING FOOTNOTE: https://blog.
hubspot.com/sales/prospecting

Chapter 12: SALES REPORTING TOOLS
FOOTNOTE: https://www.unleashedsoftware.com/blog/
why-business-reporting-is-important-for-business-success

Chapter 12: LEARNING STYLES FOOTNOTE: https://www.
time4learning.com/learning-styles/

Chapter 12: MARKETING AUTOMATION
TOOLS FOOTNOTE: https://cxl.com/blog/
marketing-automation-strategy/

Chapter 12: FOOTNOTE: HOW IS AI IMPACTING SALES
ENABLEMENT? Sources: weforum.org, Huffington Post, Gartner

Printed in Great Britain
by Amazon